THE CANNABIBLE

THE CANNABIBLE

INTRODUCTION BY Robert Connell Clarke | Jason King

TEN SPEED PRESS

Berkeley · Toronto

Author's Note

Information included on the following pages regarding the lineage of *Cannabis* strains is reported with as much certainty as is possible in this elusive field of marijuana genealogy. Even the simple question, Where does a strain come from? is tricky since its answer totally depends on how far you wish to look back. When you really get down to it, all marijuana is descendant from the one original strain that God blessed us with, believed to have originated many millennia ago somewhere in Central Asia or India. But through thousands of years of natural selection and human intervention, *Cannabis* has evolved into a truly infinite number of varieties. The question is similar to asking a person where they are from. What is really being asked here? Where were they born? Where is the last place they lived for a long time? Where do they live now? Where are their ancestors from? For example, Blueberry consists of strains from Thailand and Afghanistan but it is now generally associated with the Pacific Northwest, where it was bred; more and more, Blueberry is also being associated with Amsterdam, where seeds are sold by Dutch Passion Seed Company. In general, it is safe to assume that if you are looking at an indica, it comes from Afghanistan, or close to it. As far as sativas go, they can be from literally anywhere else. Mostly what's seen today are hybrids containing genes from both the indica and sativa gene pools. So, unless otherwise stated, information regarding where a strain is "from" indicates the area that the strain is generally associated with now.

PUBLISHER'S NOTE
We take great care to ensure that the information included in this book is accurate and presented in good faith, but no warranty is provided nor results guaranteed. This material is intended for educational and entertainment purposes only. It is advisable to seek the advice of a licensed, professional health-care provider for any condition that may require medical attention.

10

Ten Speed Press
P.O. Box 7123
Berkeley, California 94707
www.tenspeed.com

Distributed in Australia by Simon and Schuster Australia, in Canada by Ten Speed Press Canada, in New Zealand by Southern Publishers Group, in South Africa by Real Books, and in the United Kingdom and Europe by Airlift Book Company.

Cover design by Jeff Puda and Toni Tajima
Text design by Toni Tajima

Library of Congress Cataloging-in-Publication Data
King, Jason, 1971–
  The cannabible / Jason King; introduction by Robert Connell Clarke.
    p. cm.
  ISBN 1-58008-208-4 (pbk.) — ISBN 1-58008-361-7 (hardcover)
  1. Cannabis. 2. Marijuana. I. Title.
  SB295.C35 K56 2001
  633.5'3—dc21   2001004451
First printing, 2001
Printed in Hong Kong

4 5 6 7 8 9 10 — 07 06 05 04 03

This book is dedicated to the Cannabis breeders of the world,
who continually risk their freedom to create the myriad strains of
Cannabis that we all love so much. Thank You!

Acknowledgments

Thanks to: Creator, Jerry Garcia, Triple J Packin, Alan Dronkers & Sensi Seeds, DJ Short, Blue Bird coffee shop, Ed Silver, Rob Clarke, Meghan Keeffe and Annie Nelson—The C*Team, Phil Wood, Greenhouse coffee shop, *Cannabis Culture,* Woody Harrelson, "K" at Trichome Technologies, Mila, Todd McCormick, Jack Herer, Dave Frankel, Ras Noah, Janegel, Ross, Mel Frank, Willow—my mentor, Eddy I & Nicki, D&O, and all the others who couldn't be named for obvious reasons—you know who you are! Mahalo!

Table of Contents

Preface

IT'S 6 A.M. and the sound of roosters awakens me from my restful sleep. The *pakalolo*—Hawaiian for "crazy weed"—we smoked last night was so strong that I still feel stoned. After a breakfast of fresh coconuts and mangoes, I roll up a fatty of Swahili—a pure sativa from Africa—to complete my wake-and-bake ceremony. (Swahili is my favorite morning bud, for it provides a soaring and energetic high that never burns out.) I'm in the Puna District of Hawaii, and today I will be climbing to the top of fifty-foot-tall rainforest trees, strapped with forty pounds of fragile camera equipment, to photograph the legendary Puna Blueberry. After hearing of my project, the kind and trusting grower has agreed to take me to the trees to photograph his magnificent crop. After about a mile of hiking through mosquito-infested jungle, we finally reach the location. I am asked to look up and try to spot the plants. A careful scan of the rainforest canopy from below reveals nothing. "Exactly my point," says the grower, as he removes his sandals for the climb up. I feel the tree; it's wet and very slippery, even for a rainforest. "Seems kind of dangerous, wouldn't you say?" I ask. No answer. My guide, loaded with four gallons of water, scurries up the wet tree like a cat being chased. I make one last check of my gear, grab a wet branch, and start climbing.

After twenty feet or so, my heart is pounding so hard that I can hear it as I grab yet another branch. The tree is extremely slippery, but through sheer determination to live, not damage my gear, and most importantly, smoke some Blueberry, I make it to the top.

Helicopters can be heard in three different directions, so we stay hidden in the canopy for a few minutes. I can already smell the sweet blue fragrance of the fabled Blueberry, one of my favorite strains for many years now. When the coast is clear, we pop our heads up into the canopy to be greeted by ten beautiful "ladies" soaking up the hot, tropical sunlight. One squeeze reveals that this is the real Blueberry strain, a creation of breeder DJ Short.

———————————

Many factors influenced my decision to write this book. First and foremost, I realized that for almost every other plant on earth, there are books documenting the numerous varieties with color photographs and descriptions. Why, I wondered, isn't there a book like this for our favorite plant? I was more disturbed when I considered the diversity of the species in question. *Cannabis* grows in every imaginable shade of color, with infinite shapes, flavors, aromas, and effects. I have tasted more flavors in marijuana than in food. This amazing plant needed to be seen in all its glory. And urgently, because many of today's *Cannabis* strains may soon be extinct. Thus I decided to dedicate my life to properly documenting (and sampling) the world's finest *Cannabis* strains.

I packed my stuff and left the lovely island paradise of Kauai, Hawaii, that I called home at the time. In California, I collected all the necessary equipment for the job—a Canon EOS camera with a ringlight, several professional-quality lenses, a high-powered trinocular microscope, a 150-watt fiber-optic illuminator—and set on my way. I wanted to learn photomicrography (microscope photography). This was a serious challenge, as there was no school within 1,000 miles. So, I bought my first microscope and learned the hard way. *Cannabis* is extremely difficult to photograph under the microscope because of its three-dimensionality. The depth of field with a microscope is incredibly short, a fact that usually goes unnoticed because most microscope specimens are sliced thin on a slide, thus being virtually two-dimensional. This simply wouldn't work with *Cannabis;* squished onto a slide, the resin glands explode, and it's not very pretty. Eventually I had special optics designed for my microscope to increase the depth of field. Five hundred rolls of film and nearly five years later, I am on my fifth microscope and this one works beautifully.

In the five years since I began this project, it seems to have snowballed into an entire career. Phone calls, letters, and e-mails started coming from magazines and galleries around the world, requesting articles, art, and photography—all on the subject of *Cannabis.* I was more than happy to oblige, and began writing and taking photographs for several cannabis magazines including *Cannabis Culture.* I designed two cannabis-related clothing lines and created an "Exotic Marijuana" poster. These were all blessings that helped me get by while I traveled the globe, hunting down every type of marijuana to be found.

In the first two years, I photographed well over a thousand marijuana strains from all around the world. The problem was that less than two hundred were identifiable and believable in their reported lineage. Where a strain is from, where a particular sample is grown, and where the sample was obtained are often completely different factors. After four years, my list approached 1,500 strains with reputable information on approximately 250. These strains were consistently recognizable, meaning identifiable no matter where or by whom they were grown. *The Cannabible* focuses on these 250 varieties. I found them in North America, including Hawaii and Canada, and Europe—with a major emphasis on Amsterdam—the epicenters for the finest cannabis in the world.

Due to the illegality of marijuana, it was often very difficult, if not impossible, to ascertain complete information about all of the strains documented within the pages of this book. For example, let's say I came across a sample called Asian Fantasy. After questioning the dealer, I found out that this is the name he assigned to it for selling purposes. The guy he gets it from, the grower, calls it Triple A. Further questioning reveals that this grower's source, a man who has had the strain for over twenty years, calls it Cambodian #8. One can only guess what the natives in Cambodia call this strain.

I photographed marijuana everywhere from Amsterdam coffee shops to school buses, from Cannabis Buyers Clubs to the inside of a volcanic crater. These are the strains whose information I believe is accurate or that were just so beautiful I wanted to share them. I have worked diligently to get correct and current information, consulting breeders, growers, seed companies, smokers, and anyone else who seemed credible. And yet I often received conflicting stories about the different varieties, even from the most knowledgeable experts on the subject. I have sifted through this information and hereby present what I believe to be the most accurate strain descriptions anywhere. If you have more complete information on any of these plants, please e-mail me at cannabible@hotmail.com so I can include it in the next edition of *The Cannabible.* Also, despite massive efforts, I was not able to include scratch and sniffs in the book. Maybe next year. Happy drooling!

SINSEMILLA HERITAGE: What's in a Name?

by Robert Connell Clarke

Introduction

Marijuana use has become commonplace across North America and Europe. During the last two decades, domestic marijuana varietal names such as Haze, Northern Lights, and Skunk have become household words, while traditional imported products such as Acapulco Gold, Colombian Wacky Weed, Panama Red, and Thai Sticks have vanished. The diversity and quality of imported marijuana and hashish have declined markedly. What happened to these once-famous imports, and where did the new varieties come from? The effects of exuberant law enforcement on limiting the quality and variety of imported marijuana have been exceeded only by greed on the part of producers and smugglers. A marijuana trader makes a larger profit from selling a lot of lousy marijuana than from a little, good stash. These conditions have led to the widespread proliferation of the homegrown marijuana movement.

Fortunately, since 1980, Dutch marijuana seed companies have made seeds of hybrid *Cannabis* drug varieties readily available to growers everywhere. This has provided a great opportunity for myriad growers to acquire high-potency varieties that were previously unavailable. What follows is an encapsulation of the mere twenty years of modern marijuana breeding history, combining centuries of selections by indigenous farmers into varieties for years to come.

What Is Marijuana Breeding?

Marijuana breeders are growers who breed new cultivars (cultivated varieties) of marijuana. Only a very few marijuana growers create new seeds, consciously selecting and breeding their best plants in an effort to improve their varieties. The vast majority of marijuana growers practice no selection at all, and grow seeds produced from vegetative cuttings from selected female plants or even grow seeds produced accidentally.

The life cycle of *Cannabis* presents several obstacles to improvement by selective breeding. Male and female *Cannabis* flowers usually occur on separate plants, and thus *Cannabis* plants are generally incapable of self-pollinating. Self-pollinating is the most effective means of fixing desirable traits, since the selected genes are more likely to be represented in both the male pollen and the female ovule if they are born on the same plant. In marijuana breeding, the female genes controlling a selected trait must be present in two separate individual plants, one male pollen parent and one female seed parent. Both marijuana and hashish come from strictly female plants. This makes it very difficult to recognize potentially favorable traits hidden in male parents. All marijuana varieties are wind-pollinated and intercross freely, so prospective seed parents must be isolated to avoid stray pollinations until they are to be pollinated with a selected male.

Due to the illegality and high visibility of marijuana cultivation, growers prefer to limit the size of their gardens and the frequency of their visits to observe the crops. This lowers the total number of plants the breeder will have to choose from and limits the amount of time that can be spent selecting prospective parents for breeding. It is very difficult to breed marijuana successfully without a secure and stable place to develop generation after generation of offspring. When breeders lose their genetic base of seeds or cuttings, progress stops dead. All said and done, North America is a rough playing field for marijuana breeding.

History of Marijuana Breeding in North America

Varieties of marijuana originating in India have been grown throughout the Caribbean and bordering coastal nations from Mexico to Brazil since 1834, when the British brought indentured Indian servants to their Caribbean colonies. Marijuana use did not become illegal in America until 1937, and large-scale commercial importation of hashish and marijuana into Europe and North America did not commence until the early 1960s.

Marijuana growing began in North America during the 1960s. At first, seeds cleaned from illicit shipments of marijuana were casually planted by curious smokers. Sinsemilla (Spanish for "seedless") marijuana was almost unheard of. Nearly all domestically produced marijuana that lacked seeds was immature, and mature marijuana was fully seeded. Tropical varieties from Colombia and Thailand grown in North America rarely matured before frosts killed them. However, some of the tropical varieties regularly survived until maturity in coastal Florida, Southern California, and Hawaii, where the climate is warm and the growing season is long. Alternately, subtropical Mexican and Jamaican varieties often matured outdoors across the southern two-thirds of the United States. All of these early introductions were called "sativas," a common name derived from the botanical name *Cannabis sativa.*

In the early 1970s, a handful of growers began to produce sinsemilla. Seedless plants are created by removing male plants from the fields, leaving only the unfertilized female plants to mature. Instead of setting seeds in the first receptive flowers, the female plants continue to produce copious additional flowers, covered by hundreds of thousands of resin glands. By the mid 1970s, sinsemilla was becoming the primary style of domestic marijuana production.

In 1976, a coffee-table book called *Sinsemilla Marijuana Flowers* by Jim Richardson and Arik Woods revolutionized marijuana growing in North America. Not only did the authors accurately and sensitively portray the sinsemilla technique with their excellent text and lavish color photographs, they made the first attempt to describe the proper stages of floral maturity for an optimally potent and tasty harvest. Most importantly, this publication, just twenty-five years ago, suggested to growers that if marijuana can be grown without seeds, it follows that select female flowers can also be intentionally fertilized with select pollen to produce a few seeds of known parentage. This realization, in turn, gave birth to the expansion of conscious marijuana breeding and the myriad varieties portrayed in this volume.

Early on, marijuana growers worked with any varieties they could procure in the search to find potent plants that would consistently mature before being killed by frosts. Since most imported marijuana was full of seeds, many landraces (traditional cultivars grown by indigenous peoples) were available to growers. Early-maturing northern Mexican varieties proved to be favorites as they consistently finished maturing at northerly latitudes. The early-maturing North American sativa varieties of the early and mid-1970s (such as Polly and Eden Gold) resulted from hybrid crosses between Mexican or Jamaican landraces and more potent, but later-maturing Panamanian, Colombian, and Thai landraces. (In all hybrid crosses, the female seed parent is listed before the "x"—the symbol indicating a cross—and the male pollen parent is listed after the "x." If the sexual identity of the parents is unknown, a "/" symbol is used rather than the "x.") Traditional cultivars gave modern growers a strong start having been favored and selected for potent landrace varieties for hundreds of years. Even today a few special imported shipments are far more potent than the average marijuana grown in Europe or North America. However, by 1980, the best domestic North American sinsemilla was rated amongst the world's strongest.

Most varieties in the 1970s were adapted to outdoor growing, but others were specially developed for greenhouse or indoor, artificial light growing, where the season can be extended to allow late-maturing cultivars to finish. Once varieties that would mature under the given conditions were perfected, pioneering marijuana breeders selected for high potency—high delta-1-THC content with low CBD content—followed by the aesthetic considerations of flavor, aroma, and color. (Delta-1-tetrahydrocannabinol, or THC, is the primary psychoactive compound in *Cannabis.* Cannabidiol, or CBD, is not psychoactive, but may alter the effects of THC.) Modifying adjectives, such as minty, floral, spicy, fruity, sweet, purple, golden, or red, were often attached to selected varieties, and thus domestic sinsemilla connoisseurship was born. Continued inbreeding of the original favorable hybrids resulted in some of the legendary sativas of the 1970s, such as Original Haze, Purple Haze, Polly, Eden Gold, Three Way, Maui Wowie, Kona Gold, Matanuska Thunderfuck, and Big Sur Holy Weed, which were almost always grown outdoors or in greenhouses. From 1975 until the end of the decade, marijuana breeders had great success continuing to develop connoisseur sativa cultivars. Sweeter, prettier flowers brought the grower great pride and even greater profit. Purple varieties gained popularity, largely following on the coattails of the extraordinary Purple Haze of Central California.

By 1980, commercial sinsemilla cultivation had become much more common. Professional growers developed sativa varieties that were both high yielding and early maturing, and police awareness of commercial cultivation increased, especially in the western United States. Small aircraft were routinely used to search for larger marijuana plantations located in remote terrain, and many small growers were turned in to the police by snoopy, alarmist neighbors. The authorities soon learned that marijuana matures in the autumn so a variety that could be brought out of the field and into the drying shed by early October avoided some of the problems that might arise with a variety that matured in late November. Faced with storage problems resulting from numerous seizures, the authorities often merely counted seized plants and burned the bulk of the confiscated crop immediately without weighing it. Prosecution was based on the number of plants counted. Just enough dried marijuana was saved for laboratory analysis to be used as evidence in court. Concurrent with increased sinsemilla production was an increased incidence of crops being stolen. The fewer large and early-maturing plants a cultivator could grow, while continuing to realize a sufficient yield and profit, the better the chances of avoiding detection by law enforcement or thieves.

When *Cannabis* responds positively to lots of water, sun, and nutrients, it produces huge plants, sometimes yielding up to five pounds (almost two kilograms) of dried flowers. The more they are fed and watered, the taller and bushier they become, even when heavily pruned. The larger the plant, the easier it is to spot from the air or over a fence. This situation kindled a desire in growers for plants with a short, broad stature and high flower yield. Before 1975, almost all sinsemilla was grown from sativa varieties. Correctly grown Colombian, Mexican, or Thai varieties averaged over eight feet (two and one-half meters) tall when pruned or trellised, and could easily reach thirteen to sixteen feet (four to five meters) when grown unrestricted in full sun. As marijuana breeders continued to cross their shortest, earliest-maturing, and highest-yielding sativa cultivars with each other and pruned frantically, they yearned for something new. Their salvation was manifested in a new and exotic foreign variety of marijuana called "indica."

The Introduction of Indica

Most modern European and North American sinsemilla varieties are a blend of South Asian marijuana varieties called sativas that spread throughout South and Southeast Asia, Africa, and North and South America, and have been (since the 1970s) crossed with Central Asian and Middle Eastern hashish cultivars, commonly called "indicas," a name based on the botanical name *Cannabis indica.* The most well-known indica varieties came from Afghanistan and Pakistan. Indica plants are characterized as short and bushy with broad, dark green leaves, which makes them somewhat harder to see from afar. They usually mature quite early, from late August to the end of September, often stand only three to six feet (one to two meters) tall at maturity, and produce copious resin-covered leaves and flowers. At least several dozen introductions of indica seeds from Afghanistan or Pakistan into North America were made during the middle to late 1970s. Afghani No. 1, Mazar-i-sharif, and Hindu Kush were some of the earliest indica introductions and are still available today. Since the Soviet invasion of Afghanistan in 1979, many more indicas have made their way directly to Dutch seed companies from neighboring Pakistan. Indica added economically valuable traits to extant domestic marijuana varieties, but it was considered rough by many

smokers, being originally intended for bulk hashish production, rather than fine sinsemilla. Marijuana breeders still needed the traditional sativas to make hybrids that were both potent and cerebral.

Marijuana breeders intentionally crossed early-maturing indica varieties with the sweet, but later-maturing, sativa varieties to produce early-maturing hybrids. Soon the majority of growers began to try a few indica/sativa hybrids. By the early 1980s, the vast majority of all commercially produced sinsemilla in North America had likely received some portion of its genetic composition from the indica gene pool, and it had become difficult to find the pre-indica, pure sativa varieties that had been so popular only a few years earlier. There are now very few pure sativas grown in North America and Europe, as they mature late outdoors and require extra time to mature indoors, resulting in higher costs and risks. Many of the indica/sativa hybrids were vigorous growers, matured earlier, yielded well, were very potent, and were easier to conceal due to their shorter stature. Skunk No. 1 (Colombian sativa/Afghan indica x Acapulco Gold Mexican sativa) is a good example of a hybrid expressing predominantly sativa traits, and Northern Lights (Afghan indica/Thai sativa) is a good example of a hybrid expressing predominantly indica traits.

Indica hybrids spread like wildfire. Although the influence of indica generally increased steadily throughout the mid-1980s (owing to its delayed introduction in many regions), its popularity in pioneering regions had begun to decline. Since *Cannabis* is wind-pollinated and sinsemilla is usually grown in enclosed gardens, accidental pollination often results in many seeds. Accidental seeds are far more common than intentionally produced seeds, and are rapidly and widely distributed in retail sinsemilla. Intentionally produced seeds are usually only passed along from one serious breeder to another or purchased from seed companies, and their distribution is more limited. Accidentally produced seeds containing varying proportions of the introduced indica gene pool were grown and randomly crossed again and again. Such random outcrossing produced a complex hybrid condition such that favorable traits were rarely consistently reproducible. Few of the offspring looked like their siblings, their gene pools having been formed from randomly collected genetic scraps handed down from their assorted predecessors. Over the next few years, the mixed gene pools reassorted, manifesting many undesirable as well as desirable characteristics.

Without careful selection and breeding, marijuana begins to turn weedy, and as natural selection takes over, varieties lose their vigor, taste, and potency. Accidental recombination of complex hybrids brought out some of the less desirable traits of indica that were previously suppressed. Reduced potency; a slow, flat, dreary high; and a skunky, acrid aroma and harsh taste quickly became associated with many indica/sativa hybrids. Also, indica's dense, tightly packed floral clusters tend to trap moisture, encouraging gray mold, for which it has little native resistance. This often results in significant crop losses that were rarely a problem when only pure sativa varieties were grown. Indica/sativa hybrids are still what the average sinsemilla consumer purchases today. To the sinsemilla connoisseur, indica has not proven to be all it was cracked up to be. Although consumers and commercial growers of the late 1970s adopted indica enthusiastically, serious breeders of the 1980s began to view indica with more skepticism.

The average commercial or home grower, however, may express quite a different opinion. Indica's hardy growth, rapid maturation, and tolerance to cold allowed sinsemilla to be grown outdoors in the northern United States, from Washington to Maine and across southern Canada. This revolutionized the marijuana market by making potent homegrown a reality for those living at northern latitudes, as well as widening the scope and intensity of sinsemilla cultivation. Production dispersed from the U.S. epicenters of the West Coast, Hawaii, and the Ozark mountains into at least twenty major producing states. Some sinsemilla is now grown outdoors in all fifty American states, across southern Canada, and throughout much of Europe. Indica/sativa hybrids have also proven to be well-adapted to indoor cultivation. Compact indica/sativa hybrid varieties mature quickly, allowing three to four harvests per year, and yield an average of three to four ounces (one hundred grams) of dry flowers on plants only three feet tall. Sativa varieties are too stretchy and tall, take too long to mature, and the tops of the plants, near the lights, shade the bottom branches, preventing them from producing many flowers.

The introduction of indica also had a more subtle, and possibly longer-lasting, effect on sinsemilla breeding. Purple coloration had become a sign of quality and potency in late-maturing sativa cultivars like Purple Haze. The consumer's thirst for exotic purple sinsemilla created the short-lived "Purple Craze" of the early 1980s. Growers discovered that indica varieties would often turn purple if they were left out through a frost. For a year or two, many growers were able to get more money for purple flowers, but early-maturing indica varieties, when left in the field through a frost, lost much of their potency. This abruptly ended the Purple Craze, and enlightened marijuana breeders realized that many traits prove to be desirable only in certain varieties under certain conditions. The conscious breeder should be extremely selective when experimenting with new introductions.

Has indica's invasion of North America and Europe proven to be more of a bane than a boon? Is the future of domestic sinsemilla cultivation and breeding dismal and hopeless as a result of indica contamination? Although indica may currently appear to be less desirable to connoisseurs, it has certainly provided a big advantage for the average sinsemilla grower and smoker. Concerned sinsemilla breeders still produce better and better pure sativa and indica/sativa hybrid varieties. Open exchanges of information and seeds are commonplace among breeders, and connoisseur marijuana breeding will continue to progress, if ever so slowly. Unfortunately, sinsemilla breeders form close-knit groups, and most beginning growers don't know them. High-quality seeds will continue to have a more limited distribution than accidental seeds collected from retail purchases until the availability of high-quality seeds increases.

Turning the Indica Tide

In their search for high-quality genetic stock, connoisseur sinsemilla breeders have returned to some of their original pure sativa varieties. By crossing them into the now highly inbred indica/sativa hybrid varieties, breeders can enhance the hybrid's flavor and boost its potency. Breeders are continually searching for new sources of exotic seeds. Pure unhybridized indica varieties are still highly prized breeding material, and new indica introductions are occasionally received from Afghanistan and Pakistan. Sativa varieties from South Africa have recently gained favor with outdoor growers, as they mature early but don't suffer from many of the aesthetic drawbacks of indica. Pure South African varieties, originating far south of the equator, often mature in August, but are shorter in stature, moderately potent, and relatively high yielding. Hybrid crosses between indicas and classic indica/sativa hybrid varieties such as Skunk No. 1 are usually vigorous and early maturing and may express the desirable sativa and indica traits of high potency, fine fragrance, and high yield.

Prior to 1980, a few breeders also worked with weedy sativa varieties from Central Europe. Most Western growers call these varieties "ruderalis." These weedy varieties begin maturing in July or early August, which hastens the maturity of outdoor hybrid marijuana varieties. Unfortunately, they are almost entirely devoid of THC and are high in CBD. Potency suffers in hybrid offspring, and subsequent selections must be made to restore high levels of psychoactivity. However, the biggest problem with weedy varieties and their hybrids is that they are not determinate. A single plant will continue to produce new flowers until it is harvested, rather than all of its flowers maturing before harvest, so its full potential is never realized. Ruderalis hybrids will likely prove of great value only to outdoor growers at near polar latitudes where little else will grow.

North American breeders also used other exotic imports to impart particular flavors to the smoke or to enhance the potency of hybrids. Landrace varieties from Brazil, India, Indonesia, Kashmir, Korea, Nepal, Africa, and other far-flung locations were occasionally used for these purposes. Since commercial shipments of marijuana did not often originate from these regions, usually the seeds were collected in small numbers and were relatively rare compared to seeds from the major marijuana-producing regions such as Colombia, Mexico, Jamaica, and Thailand. Presently, it is nearly impossible to import seeds from new, potent, imported varieties. They rarely can be collected as there are very few locations remaining where indigenous farmers maintain traditional high-potency landraces. Basically, we are stuck with what we have in circulation, like it or not, and breeders must make the best of what they have.

A few strong branches of the North American marijuana family tree were transplanted to the Netherlands, and the remaining scions continued to flourish and evolve, leading to the tremendous diversity of marijuana varieties grown in North America and Europe today. Resulting from the openness of marijuana seed sales in the Netherlands, Dutch seed companies provide an easily documented model of the sinsemilla breeding that has continued simultaneously in North America. The Dutch seed companies described much of the heritage behind their varieties in their early catalogs. The following information comes directly from published seed catalogs and is supplemented with personal comments from breeders and seed company owners.

Dutch Seed Companies

During the early 1980s, several marijuana seed companies appeared in the Netherlands, where cultivation of *Cannabis* for seed production and the sale of seeds were tolerated. Political pressure on marijuana growers in North America forced the thrust of progress in sinsemilla breeding to the Netherlands, where the political climate was much less threatening. For North American and European growers, this meant continued availability of exotic high-quality marijuana seeds.

Almost all of the Dutch varieties contain germ plasm from one or more of the founding genetic building blocks brought from North America. Cultivars such as Original Haze,

Hindu Kush, Afghani No. 1, and Skunk No. 1 were established in California before their seeds were taken to the Netherlands in the early 1980s. As these cultivars were relatively stable seed varieties, breeders had a greater chance of selecting a favorable male plant as a pollen source for breeding. Cultivars such as Northern Lights, Big Bud, Hash Plant, and G-13 went to the Netherlands from the Pacific Northwest as rooted female cuttings. There were never males of these varieties, and, therefore, commercial seeds were all made by crosses with a male of a different variety such as Skunk No. 1, or more rarely by masculinizing a female cutting to produce pollen for self-pollinating.

When connoisseurs of North American sinsemilla comment that "All the Dutch varieties seem the same," this should come as no surprise, since Dutch varieties share so much of their heritage. Of the nearly 150 varieties offered for sale by Dutch seed companies in 2000, 80 percent of them contain germ plasm that first came to the Netherlands prior to 1985. Most of the seed companies have continued to reshuffle the heavily stacked deck of original North American germ plasm, and since the 1980s few companies have introduced anything new. The perpetuation of monotony has been punctuated, only infrequently, by new introductions from North America or traditional marijuana-producing nations. Most seed companies have simply recombined founding cultivars from which breeders selected star clones to represent their seed companies in competitions. What goes around, comes around!

But where would we be today without the common building blocks of our common varieties? Many varieties have been tried throughout the years, and the persistence of the original founding germ plasm to this day is testimony to its desirability. If more potent, better tasting, and more productive varieties had been introduced, growers would certainly favor them today. In fact, seed companies generally introduce a new variety by simply crossing a new introduction with an established Dutch variety, itself built upon the initial founding varieties, and give the resulting plant a new name. As only a handful of North American varieties were used to make "Dutch" sinsemilla varieties, they are usually potent and commercially lucrative, but often boring!

The founding blocks of germ plasm used in most Dutch sinsemilla cultivars are described below by seed company, cultivar name, date of introduction, origin, and genetic heritage. Table 1 provides early Dutch seed company cultivar histories for additional information about their specific heritage.

1979

Sacred Seeds established in California

Lowland Seed Co. established

1980

Sacred Seeds: SKUNK NO.I, AFGHANI NO. I, HINDU KUSH, and ORIGINAL HAZE

1981-1983

Lowland Seed Co.: Zukke Knolle, H 12, M 7, and Ewcc-superseeds

1984

Dr. Wiet Exotic Seed Co. established

Sinsemilla Seed Co. established: HASH PLANT NO.I, Hungarian RUDERALIS, Skunk No.I, Afghani No.I, Purple Skunk, Mazar-i-Sharif Afghani, Gold Colombian, Indonesian, Indian, JAMAICAN, Malawi, Oaxaca Mexican, Pokhara Nepalese, Nigerian, Panama Red, South African, and Thai imported seed; Skunk No.2, Oregon Indica, Dutch Oregon Indica, Early Flowering Indica Sweet Smelling, Purple Variety; Oregon Indica, Krazy Karol and Kashroc "stabilized" varieties; Kerala South Indian sativa x Afghani indica, Thai x Mexican, Afghani x Mexican, Indian x Mexican, Thai x Afghani, Nigerian x Afghani, Jamaican x Afghani, and Afghani No.I/Skunk No.I hybrids

1985

Cultivator's Choice: CALIFORNIA ORANGE, EARLY GIRL, SOUTH AFRICAN or DURBAN POISON, Mazari Afghani, INDI-SAT and Acapulco Gold "stabilized" varieties, and Durban Poison x Skunk No.I hybrid

Super Sativa Seed Club established: CHITRAL INDICA [aka Chitral], Manila Filipino, Nigerian, Durban [aka Durban Poison], Primo Hollanditis, Oakland Indica, The Creeper and Khyber Afghani, Afghani/Nepali, Purple Rain, Friesland Indica, Gouda's Glory, Amsterdam Delight and Mexican x Skunk No.I, Durban x Thai, Durban x Brazilian, Durban x Chitral Indica, Chitral Indica x Tuguegaro Filipino, Skunk No.I x Basic 5, Pakistan x Ruderalis, Kandahar Indica, Indica x Creeper, Kandahar Indica x Michuacan, Nigerian x Kandahar Indica, Khyber Afghani x Nigerian Afghani/Nepali x Northern Mexican, Afghani/Nepali x Kerala, Afghani x Malawi, Tirah Nepali x Thai, Khyber Afghani x Kerala, and Khyber Afghani x Creeper hybrids

Seed Bank: NORTHERN LIGHTS

1986

Positronics: Skunk USA, Phillip's delight, Dr. Wiet's Own, Afghaan, NOI (Nederlandse Oregon-Indica Old Ed's variety) and Paars Purple "stabilized" varieties, and Paars Purple x Nat. Seed hybrid

SSSC: WILLIAMS WONDER, Skunk No.I and Afghani No. I, Early Bird, Victor Baarn, Royal Dutch, Lone Ranger, Beatrix Choice "stabilized" varieties; Afghani No.I x Skunk No.I and Creeper x Skunk No.I hybrids

Seed Bank: Early Girl, EARLY PEARL [aka Early Girl x Pollyanna], Early Skunk, California Orange, Indisat and South African D.P. 34 [aka Durban Poison] "stabilized" varieties; Early Pearl x Mazar-i-Sharif, Northern Lights #9 x Skunk No.I, Northern Lights #? x Afghani No.I hybrids and a Shady Lady-Ruderalis x Afghani No.I hybrid

1987

Dr. Wiet Exotic: Dr. Wiet x Skunk Mix, Skunk Mix, Dr. Wiet Mix, Dr. Wiet Purple Mix, and Dr. Wiet Kwekers Mix

Positronics: HOLLANDSCH HOOP [aka Holland's Hope] and First Girl [aka Early Girl]

SSSC: Heavenly High, Hawaiian, Pakistani, and Hoosier, Hoot'n Hollar introduced from the U.S.

Dutch Passion established: AMSTEL GOLD, PURPLE STAR, PURPLE WONDER, FOUR-WAY, and Skunk No. I

Seed Bank: Northern Lights #1 x ?, Northern Lights #5 x Northern Lights #2?, Northern Lights #5 x Skunk No.I, Northern Lights #1 x Skunk No.I/Afghani, Big Bud (Big Bud x Skunk No.I?] and Pollypak hybrids; Big Bud x Big Bud/Northern Lights and Hash Plant [aka Hash Plant x Hash Plant/Northern Lights #I] back crosses and Ruderalis hybrids

1988

Seed Bank: SHIVA Skunk [aka Northern Lights #5 x Skunk No.I], G-13 x Northern Lights #2/?, Hash Plant x Northern Lights/?, G-13 x Hash Plant/?, Swazi land, and South African landrace seed; Big Skunk [aka Big Bud x Skunk No.I], Haze x Northern Lights #1/?, Northern Lights #5 x Northern Lights #2/?, and Hash Plant/Northern Lights #1/? x Swaziland hybrids

1989

SSSC: Super Indoor Indica, Super Indoor Sativa, Sonora Super Sativa and Pluton 2 "stabilized" varieties, and Haze x South African hybrid

Seed Bank: HINDU KUSH, HAWAIIAN INDICA [aka Hawaiian Indica No.7 x (Northern Lights/?)], Hash Plant, Early Pearl/Skunk No.I/Northern Lights #5 x Haze, Silver Pearl [aka Northern Lights #5 x (Early Pearl x Skunk No.I)], Silver Haze [aka Silver Pearl x Haze], and Northern Lights #2 x Skunk No.I hybrids

1990

Exotic Seed Co.: Four Way, Royal Dutch Skunk, Four and More, Dr. Weed Indica, Dr. Weed Indica Purple, Indica Northern Lights

Seed Bank: Ruderalis Skunk and Super Skunk [aka Afghani No.I x Skunk No.I]

1991-1992

Dr. Weed Seeds: Amstel Gold, Ruderalis, Dr. Weed Skunk Ruderalis, Dr. Weed Skunk Northern Lights, Skunk Indica, Twilicht, Nightqueen, Purple Nr 1, and Purple Star

Dutch Passion seeds from *Dr. Weed:* Dutch Passion Indica, < Skunk No.I, Skunk Passion Four Way Skunk, Dutch Passion Four > and More, Hindu Kush, Early Girl, South African, Haze/Skunk, Dutch Passion Northern Lights, and Big Bud Skunk

Sensi Seeds and *Sensi Seed Bank:* Shiva Shanti I, Shiva Shanti 2, Sensi Skunk, and African Queen

1993-1994

Kulu Trading: Skunk No.I, Durban Poison x Skunk No.I, Afghani No.I x Skunk No.I, Thai landrace x Skunk No.I, California Orange x Skunk No.I, Hawaiian Indica No.7 x Skunk No.I, Hindu Kush x Skunk No.I, Swaziland African landrace x Skunk No.I and Early Cal x Skunk No.I

Dutch Passion: Master Kush, Chitral, and Oasis [aka Northern Lights #2]

1995-1996

Super Skunky established

Sensi Seed Bank: Four Way, Jack Herer [aka (Northern Lights #? x Skunk No.I) x Haze], California Indica, and Juicy Fruit

1997

Super Skunky · Super Widow: Bud Bunnie, Magic Crystal, Starlight, Stoney High, Pyramid, Widow Warrior, Super Widow's Dream, Star Chief, and Easy Rider [all hybrids with a White Widow male]

Sensi Seed Bank: Black Domina

1998

Flying Dutchmen established

Dutch Passion: BLUEBERRY [aka Original Blueberry], FLO, Euforia [aka Skunk No.I], Buddha [aka (Haze x Oasis/Shiva) x (Skunk No.I x Oasis/Shiva)], Lambsbread/Skunk, Green Spirit [aka (Big Bud x ?) x Skunk No.I], Smokey Bear, Hempstar, White Cloud, and Mindbender

Sensi Seed Bank: Jack Flash [aka Jack Herer x (Super Skunk x Haze)]

1999-2000

Flying Dutchmen: The Pure [aka Skunk No.I], Early Durban [aka Durban Poison x Skunk No.I], California Sunrise [aka ? x Skunk No.I], Kabul Baba [aka Afghani No.I x Skunk No.I], Thai-tanic [aka Thai landrace x Skunk No.I], Dutchman's Royal Orange [aka California Orange x Skunk No.I], Fuma con Dios [aka ? x Skunk No.I], Pot of Gold [aka Hindu Kush x Skunk No.I], The Real McCoy [aka Hawaiian Indica No.7 x Skunk No.I], Swazi Safari [aka Swaziland African landrace x Skunk No.I], Twister [aka ? x Skunk No.I], Early California [aka Early Cal x Skunk No.I], The Original Haze [aka Original Haze x Skunk No.I], and Pure Thai [aka Thai landrace]

Dutch Passion: Holland's Hope, California Orange, Oasis [aka (Northern Lights #2 x ?) x ?], Orange Bud [aka Skunk No.I], Super Haze [aka Haze x Skunk No.I], Chitral [aka Pakistani indica landrace x Skunk No.I], Amstel Gold, Purple Star, Master Kush [aka Hindu Kush x Hindu Kush], Purple Passion or Passion #I, Power Plant [aka Durban South Africa], Mazar [aka Afghani No. I x Skunk No. I], Blue Moonshine, Blue Heaven, and Original Blue Velvet

Sensi Seed Bank: MAPLE LEAF INDICA [from Afghanistan?], Mr. Nice [aka G-13) x Hash Plant], Jamaican Pearl [aka Jamaican x Early Pearl], Durban Marley's Collie [aka Jamaican x Maple Leaf Indica], and Skunk Kush [aka Hindu Kush x Skunk No.I]

TABLE I. The seminal six seed companies operated throughout the 1980s, and many of their cultivars are still available today.

Among the earliest Dutch varieties were Holland's Hope and Amstel Gold, which were introduced in the early 1980s and are still available today. Although these predominantly indica cultivars are not very potent, they mature much earlier than most varieties, as they were bred to grow outdoors in the Netherlands. Both were bred from selections of imported Afghan hashish landraces.

The following eight cultivars were brought to the Netherlands from California as named seed varieties and were released by Cultivator's Choice seed company between 1980 and 1983. They were relatively consistent when inbred or crossed and now make up part of more than two-thirds of the varieties offered by Dutch seed companies. Many of the Cultivator's Choice varieties have been faithfully maintained since their introductions and are presently offered by the Flying Dutchman seed company.

- Skunk No. 1 kick started the high-quality Dutch homegrown scene. Even today, nearly half of the varieties sold by Dutch seed companies have Skunk No. 1 in their background. Skunk No. 1 was first introduced in the Netherlands in the late 1970s, and immediately revolutionized Dutch marijuana growing. The Dutch, basically a hashish-smoking culture, attempted to grow marijuana both outdoors and in greenhouses throughout the 1970s. Mostly, their efforts met with little popular success and *Nederwiet,* literally "low weed," was considered a joke among serious smokers. Skunk No. 1 changed everything. Under Dutch greenhouse conditions, Skunk No. 1 regularly matured and consistently produced high yields of potent buds, even when crops were grown from seed. Skunk No. 1 was originally a three-way hybrid combination between a Colombian/Afghan hybrid and an imported Mexican Acapulco Gold plant. This combination was inbred in California for several generations until the stable combination known as Skunk No. 1 resulted. Although indica makes up a quarter of Skunk No. 1 and contributes to its branchiness and compact bud structure, Skunk No. 1 is primarily a sweet-smelling sativa hybrid rather than an acrid-smelling indica, so the name "Skunk" is actually somewhat misleading. Despite its general uniformity, there are several different bud forms in Skunk No. 1, ranging from red, hairy buds with small bracts to large bracts with copious resin glands.
- The Original Haze is a late-maturing variety from Central California and was almost always grown in greenhouses, allowing it to finish in December or January. Original Haze was always connoisseur stash, and even in the 1970s it sold for as much as $200

an ounce. Original Haze is a pure sativa stabilized hybrid arising from crossing all of the best females with a male of a different imported sativa variety each year. Starting with Colombian/Mexican hybrids grown from seeds from the first crop, a South Indian male plant was used as a pollen source the second year, and a Thai male plant was used the third year. Depending on which year Haze seeds were collected, they resembled either Colombian, South Indian, or Thai plants. Original Haze varies in taste from citrus Thai notes through the gamut of sativa highlights to the deep spicy purple Colombian flavor most common in Dutch Haze cultivars. Although Haze has been available in the Netherlands since the early 1980s, it gained wide popularity only in the mid 1990s. Increasing levels of connoisseurship led to higher prices for exotic and flavorful (but later maturing and more costly to produce) Haze hybrids in preference to the redundant plethora of Dutch Skunk/Northern Lights type buds. Original Haze presently makes up part of about 15 percent of varieties available in the Netherlands, and its frequency is steadily increasing.

- Both Afghani No. 1 and Hindu Kush are pure indica landraces from Afghanistan. Initially selected for dense buds and copious resin, they are true-to-type Afghan primo hashish varieties.

- Early California is a very early maturing indica/sativa hybrid introduced in the early 1980s from California. It is relatively true breeding and stable.

- California Orange is another California indica/sativa hybrid well-known for its distinctive orange color and flavor.

- Hawaiian Indica is a strongly indica, indica/sativa hybrid that has been used in several Dutch hybrids. Its primary traits are very large bracts and copious resin production.

- Early Girl is a well-known commercial California seed variety from the late 1970s. It is generally leafy and of moderate potency, but it consistently matures early. It was included in a number of the early Dutch hybrids.

The following five cultivars were brought to the Netherlands from the Pacific Northwest as female cuttings and were introduced by the Sinsemilla Seed Company in the early 1980s. The Sinsemilla Seed Company is now known as the Sensi Seed Bank and continues to offer many hybrids bred from these original North American varieties. As there were no males of these female clones, they were always crossed with another variety in order to make seeds.

- Northern Lights was well established as a Pacific Northwest indoor seed variety by 1978 and arrived in the Netherlands as four sister clones. Northern Lights lines eventually came to incorporate Skunk No. 1 and Haze varieties around 1980. Northern Lights was mostly used as a crossing partner to provide the furry resin look often associated with potent varieties. However, Northern Lights also tends to have very small resin heads, both in comparison to the length of the gland stalks and in relation to other sinsemilla varieties. Northern Lights is found in at least 10 percent of Dutch varieties.

- Big Bud was established in the Pacific Northwest as a commercial indoor clone and was brought to the Netherlands in the mid-1980s. It is predominantly an indica-type indica/sativa hybrid and has very large, if at times leafy, buds.

- Hash Plant is a Lebanese/Thai hybrid. It was originally offered by the Super Sativa Seed Club, but the Sinsemilla Seed Company cutting was brought from North America. It is a very strongly indica hybrid variety.

- G-13 is a clone allegedly spirited away from the U.S. government pot farm in Mississippi. It is also a very strong, nearly pure indica variety.

- Ruderalis seed was collected from weedy roadside plants in Hungary by the Sinsemilla Seed Company and was used for breeding in an attempt to develop early-maturing varieties. Although hybrids with Skunk No. 1 and other North American cultivars began to flower very early, they also expressed their weedy background, never stopped flowering, and matured unevenly.

The Name Game

Tracing the varieties used by the seminal six Dutch seed companies (see Table 1) is relatively straightforward. Seed catalogs usually tell the customer what landrace or North American varieties were used to create the seeds, and the founding germ plasm was often shared by several seed companies. With the appearance of more than ten new seed companies during the early 1990s, the situation became more complex. Seed catalogs often changed the names of the varieties used in breeding or omitted the pedigree information altogether. Competition between seed companies heated up, fueled largely by *High Times* magazine's annual Cannabis Cup. The new companies were associated with some of the original companies and often incorporated the traditional varieties into their own cultivars, while also introducing new varieties that were quickly adopted by rival companies. Several seed companies appeared for only a year or two, and many others began to resell seeds produced by the major companies. It is easy to buy another company's seeds and change the variety name, making it appear to be a new and different variety. Some companies mistakenly sold seeds resulting from crossing two hybrid plants, resulting in great variability, with few, if any, of the offspring resembling either parental combination. The most common and successful way for seed companies to create new varieties was to simply cross a good female plant from an existing variety with a Skunk No. 1 male. In general, the 1990s were characterized more by a reshuffling of the original deck of varieties than by new introductions of landrace or North American varieties.

Unfortunately, some early Dutch breeders made very poor selections from the initial seeds they were given. The most common bad selection was for copious red hairs instead of for large bracts. Red hairs are a sign that female flowers are present, but they are not in themselves psychoactive. A preponderance of red hairs indicates many, but tiny, flowers with little surface area for psychoactive resin glands to develop. Second, selection for dense buds having a good retail appearance led to the proliferation of nested bracts that feel hard when squeezed, but once again lack sufficient surface area to develop copious resin glands. The third common erroneous selection was for fuzzy-looking resin glands with long sparkly stalks, but small resin heads. All three of these unfavorable traits occasionally reappear in modern Dutch varieties and should be avoided.

Sometimes crosses have been released as new varieties, with a lot of introductory hype about something new and exotic before being tested by growers. When the new crosses are actually grown, they often prove to be substandard. These so-called "varieties" usually disappear quickly because growers give them bad ratings. Most of the consistently popular cultivars have been around for several years, and many are still available today. Take a look at *Strainbase,* hosted by Overgrow.com, for dialogue between growers about sinsemilla varieties.

Fortunately, some of the more recent introductions from North America are markedly different from the previously available Dutch varieties. The T. H. Seeds company, formerly known as the C.I.A. or the K.G.B., introduced several North American varieties in the mid-1990s. The most interesting of these is S.A.G.E., which is a Haze-based variety from the coastal mountains of Big Sur, California. S.A.G.E. stands for "Sativa Afghanica Genetic Equilibrium," which is an appropriate explanation of the genetic background of many

1989 — *Homegrown Fantaseeds* established

1990–1991

1992 — *Homegrown Fantaseeds:* Haze 19 x Skunk [aka Haze x Skunk No.1]

1993 — *T. H. Seeds* established

1994
- *T. H. Seeds* ORIGINAL BUBBLEGUM
- *Serious Seeds* established: CHRONIC, BUBBLE GUM, and AK-47
- *Sagarmatha Seeds* established
- *K. C. Brains* established

1995
- *T. H. Seeds* S.A.G.E.
- *Serious:* KALI MIST [aka Haze hybrid]
- *Greenhouse Seeds* established: WHITE WIDOW [aka Brazilian?/South Indian?]
- *Seeds of Courage* established: Soma Skunk Mix seed from the U.S.
- *Paradise Seeds* established

1996
- *Serious:* White Russian [aka AK-47 x White Widow]
- *Greenhouse:* White Rhino [aka Afghani? x White Widow]
- *Seeds of Courage:* Soma Skunks #1, #5, #9, and #10; A+, Wide, and V

1997
- *T. H. Seeds:* AKORN
- *Greenhouse:* Great White Shark or Peacemaker [aka Super Skunk x White Widow and Super Silver Haze [aka (Northern Lights #5 x Haze) x Skunk No.1]
- *Seeds of Courage:* Northern Lights #5 x Haze
- *Paradise Seeds* Sensi Star

1998
- *Homegrown Fantaseeds:* Viking, Outdoor Green, Holland's Hope, Purple High, B-52, K2, Homegrown Fantasy, Shiva, Top 44, Haze, Original Misty, Super Chrystal, and First Lady
- *T. H. Seeds:* CHOCOLATE CHUNK, STINKY PINKY, MENDOCINO MADNESS, and HEAVY DUTY FRUITY [aka indica hybrids from the U.S.]
- *Greenhouse:* El Niño [aka (Haze/Super Skunk) x White Widow and Neville's Haze [aka Haze/(Northern Lights #5/Haze)]
- *Paradise:* Amsterdam Flame, Nebula [aka Haze hybrid?], Dutch Dragon, and Durga Mata [aka Super Shiva]
- *Sagarmatha:* SPECIAL K, EARLY RISER, YUMBOLT, WESTERN WINDS, STONEHEDGE [aka CAMBODIAN x WESTERN WINDS], BLUE VELVET, Slyder [aka Afghani? x (Northern Lights/?)], Flo [aka Flow], and Blueberry [aka Original Blueberry]
- *Seeds of Courage:* Haze Heaven [aka (Northern Lights x Haze) x AFGHANI/HAWAIIAN] and Free Tibet, Big Kahuna, White Light, White Willow, Afghan Delight, and Citrus Dreams [aka all from the '97 Soma Skunk series x AFGHANI/HAWAIIAN]
- *K. C. Brains:* K.C. 33 [aka (early Dutch x Thai) x BRAZIL], Haze Special [aka Haze], LÊDA UNO [aka (Brazil x K.C. 33) x K.C. 606], SWEET DREAMS [aka (Big Bud x Skunk No.1) x K.C. 606], MANGO [aka (K.C. Special Select x K.C. 33) x Afghani?], MIND BENDER [aka (Double K.C. 2 x K.C. 33) x Afghani], CRYSTAL PARADISE [aka (Big Bud x Skunk No.1) x Brasil], SWISS-XT [aka Double K.C. 2 x Mr. Swiss], WHITE K.C. [aka Real White Lady x K.C. 606], SPONTANICA [aka Secret Project No.1 x K.C. 33], BRASIL x K.C. [aka Brazil x K.C. 606], T.N.R. [aka Old Thai Dutch x Double K.C. 2], K.C. 36, Cyber Crystal, Afghani Special [aka Afghani], California Special [aka Skunk], and Northern Lights Special [aka Northern Lights]

1999–2000
- *Homegrown Fantaseeds:* Purple Power and Masterkush
- *Sagarmatha:* MATANUSKA TUNDRA [aka Matanuska Thunderfuck hybrid?], FLOW [aka Flo x Matanuska Tundra], BLUE THUNDER [aka Blueberry x Matanuska Tundra], Pole Cat, Mongolian Indica, Peak 19, and Wonderberry [aka (Bubblegum/Blueberry) x Williams Wonder]
- *Greenhouse:* HIMALAYAN GOLD [aka NEPALESE x NORTH INDIAN] and Red Devil
- *Paradise:* Sweet Purple, Sheherezade [aka Afghani?], and Belladonna [aka Super Skunk]

T.H. Seeds, Serious Seeds, Seeds of Courage, and *K.C. Brains* also continue to sell many of the popular varieties they developed before 1999.

TABLE 2. Many second generation seed companies appeared during the 1990s, and most of them continue to sell seeds.
Look here and in Table 1 to find the commercial source and origin of some of your favorite varieties.

stabilized indica/sativa hybrids. Bubblegum is a well-known seed variety from Indiana that came to Amsterdam via New England in the early 1990s. Akorn, Heavy Duty Fruity, Mendocino Madness, and Stinky Pinky are all indica/sativa hybrids introduced as female cuttings.

Most recently, a series of well-known outdoor cultivars from the Pacific Northwest has been introduced by Dutch Passion and Sagarmatha seed companies. They come from a single breeder and are called Flo, Blueberry, and Blue Velvet.

Brazilian landrace accessions apparently weigh heavily in many of the selections from the K. C. Brains seed company and in White Widow offered by the Greenhouse. The White Widow series may also have come as seeds to the Netherlands from the southeastern United States. Often a seed buyer cannot determine a variety's heritage because the lineage is concealed or unknown. At harvest time, what matters most is whether the cultivar was appropriate for the grower and growing conditions, rather than simply its supposed heritage or fancy name. Many of these excellent new varieties hold great promise for the future as breeders continue to fine-tune them for indoor, artificial light growing.

What's in a Seed?

Indica/sativa hybrids are a blend of two markedly different gene pools, so how do we classify a hybrid? Is it mostly indica, or mostly sativa? Pure indica varieties are characterized as stout, dark green, and leafy with broad leaflets and compact buds. Often they have large bracts and lots of resin glands covering both the bracts and small leaves. Occasionally the bracts of indicas are nested together inside each other. Indicas were originally used for hashish production, where the yield of resin is the most important selection criterion, even above potency.

Pure sativa varieties are tall, slim, and often light green with narrow leaflets and more lax buds. The best ones have very large individual bracts, and nested bracts are rarely seen. Resin glands are abundant, but are restricted more to the bracts and only the smallest leaflets. Sativas were originally selected for sinsemilla production, where the selection criteria of flavor and aroma are of equal importance to high potency.

When looking at a Haze bud, its pure sativa background is obvious, as is the pure indica background of a Hindu Kush. Determining the heritage of indica/sativa hybrids by simply looking at them is much more difficult. Skunk No. 1 is three-quarters sativa, but the more apparent indica traits of large compact buds and highly branched growth mask many of the more subtle sativa traits, making it difficult to see its strongly sativa heritage.

A few of the seed company catalogs still list the genetic background of their cultivars. When tracing the heritage of sinsemilla varieties, it is important to learn which pollen source was used, as the male will determine half of the genetic composition of the resultant seeds. Seed varieties are usually named for only the female clonal seed parent, and only a few seed companies grow their seeds to maturity to test them for consistency of quality. Similarly, sinsemilla sold in Dutch coffee shops as a certain variety is nearly always produced from the mother clone bearing that varietal name (which is used as the seed parent), rather than from Dutch-produced seeds purchased by a grower. Experienced growers prefer to know the backgrounds of both the female and the male parent.

The most important criterion for judging any seed company is the consistency of its seed varieties. If you grow Big Boy tomatoes once, you want seeds called Big Boy to produce Big Boy tomatoes the next time you buy them. This is also true of marijuana varieties, but to a lesser degree. If a grower buys Haze seeds, the offspring are expected to mature late and smell and taste like a characteristic Haze. Most seed companies carefully maintain a genetic library of both female and male parental clones, from which they can select a seed and a pollen parent to make reproducible seeds of a specified cultivar each time a fresh batch of seeds is needed. Some companies, such as Dr. Wiet's Exotic Seeds, employed a population approach to maintain varieties by using several females and males as parents in each generation. This approach led to variable and unpredictable results. Although variety may be the spice of life, too much variety leads to the erosion of varietal identity. Some seed companies have begun to sell all-female seeds resulting from a cross between a female plant and a female plant with male flowers. These crosses result in all or nearly all female offspring, but the populations are not always uniform for other characteristics.

Some of the early introductions from traditional foreign sources and North America were considered pure, consistent, stable, or true-breeding varieties. This means that when crossed with other varieties, the results were relatively predictable, at least much more so than with recently hybridized varieties. In the traditional marijuana varieties, this consistency and predictability resulted from repeated natural selection by the environment, intercrossing within populations, or incest breeding between individual sibling plants under human selection for favorable traits that eventually became present throughout the landrace. Modern sinsemilla cultivars were initially derived from hybrid crosses and stabilized by incest breeding of male and female siblings over several generations. Thus, many modern cultivars are blends of various landrace populations, selected year after year for their combined favorable traits until a majority of offspring express the entire suite of favorable traits. These inbred lines, or IBLs, are relatively true-breeding and form the cornerstones of any successful seed company. In essence, modern breeders accelerated the age-old natural process whereby landraces are created.

Because marijuana is a difficult plant in which to fix traits through selective breeding, and only the female plants are of economic importance, it is advantageous to clone exceptional plants by rooting cuttings. In this way, practically unlimited numbers of identical female plants can be grown from one select seedling. Besides circumventing the vagaries of genetic recombination, cloning can produce uniform crops of female plants in one generation. No removal of male plants is required to produce sinsemilla, as only female plants are cloned. All the flowers mature at the same time, and the whole crop can be harvested at once. This is an obvious boon to commercial sinsemilla cultivation. Clones of valuable male plants can also be preserved for breeding programs. Due to continuing governmental pressure against outdoor growers, more and more sinsemilla production has moved indoors. Artificial lighting systems are often set up in attics, bedrooms, or basements, where space is limited. These conditions don't allow room for nonproductive plants, so the single best clone is usually selected for all future cultivation. Only a few seeds are required to grow a handful of female plants, just one or two of which really need to excel. The best plants can be vegetatively reproduced and grown commercially without introducing any more seeds. In this case, it is actually an advantage to have an acceptable degree of uniformity, combined with a bit of variety so a truly superior plant can be selected for cloning. Female clones improve grow-room yields but preclude the possibility of seed production. Growers rarely practice breeding now, and variety improvement has slowed. It is difficult to say whether cloning will have a lasting effect on *Cannabis* breeding and evolution, but my guess is it will continue to limit diversity in sinsemilla cultivars.

The Future of the Dutch Seed Scene

Over the past twenty years, Dutch seed companies have made seeds of high-quality marijuana cultivars available to growers worldwide. Without the Dutch influence, North American and European sinsemilla production would not have become what it is today. Over 150 cultivars are offered in current seed catalogs, and most of them have been available for several years. However, the price of Dutch seeds has increased wildly over the past two decades. The Sinsemilla Seed Company first sold imported landrace seeds for twenty-five cents each and hybrids for fifty cents. Current catalogs reflect prices for hybrid seeds ranging from one to over ten dollars each! It is difficult to imagine that the cost of production has increased so drastically or that the quality of the seeds has improved tenfold, especially since these modern varieties share so much heritage. The success of Dutch seed sales has led to the establishment of retail seed companies in Britain, Canada, Germany, Switzerland, and other countries where marijuana seed sales are somewhat tolerated. Presently, over four hundred named varieties are available from nearly one hundred companies around the world.

However, even the sanctuary of the Netherlands has recently undergone major changes. Since March 2000, marijuana seed cultivation is no longer allowed under Dutch law. Previously, it was legal to grow any variety of fiber or drug *Cannabis* for seed in any environment. Now, it is only legal to grow *Cannabis* outdoors for seed or fiber; it may not be cultivated in greenhouses or under artificial lights. This means that seed companies will be prosecuted if they are caught with an indoor seed crop. The maximum penalty for marijuana growing has also been increased from two to four years. Some seed companies grow sinsemilla for the Dutch coffee shop trade, and it is difficult to predict how the new laws will affect them. At least one major company has ceased production and will rely on available seed supplies until they run out. One thing is sure, the availability and variety of seeds may decrease, but their price certainly will not.

Largely in response to aggressive law enforcement, coupled with the popularity and limited availability of high-quality marijuana, the trend for individuals to grow their own sinsemilla, whether for personal use or commercial profit, is spreading rapidly across North America and Europe. Marijuana smoking and cultivation for personal use may be widely legalized or tolerated eventually, if not through the public openly favoring legalization, then by increasing awareness of the inherent futility of marijuana prohibition. Suppression of personal choice will continue, but widespread tolerance is inevitable. The continued availability of high-quality seeds has largely determined the path for future development of the sinsemilla scene. High-quality sinsemilla varieties have been spread far and wide for decades. No matter what happens to Dutch seed companies, sinsemilla will still be grown, consumers will continue to smoke it, and the market will expand.

GALLERY

AFGHANI

Marijuana from Afghanistan is generally called Afghani. This is what we commonly refer to as indica, although a more accurate name would be *C. Afghanica*. Interestingly, the word *indica* was originally used to refer to Indian sativa. Afghani plants are characterized as short and squat, with wide, dark green leaves that have very wide individual leaflets. These plants, which are rarely over six feet tall, usually pump out copious amounts of resin. They are normally used for making hash. In the '70s, most of the marijuana smoked was sativa. Then, as Afghanica was introduced, it was bred into just about everything, due to its highly desirable traits. Today, it's in just about every strain on the planet. It should be noted that any strain from Afghanistan is an indica, while everything else is a sativa. Afghani buds are usually acrid and hashy, sometimes even skunky. The high is of narcotic quality, heavy and lethargic.

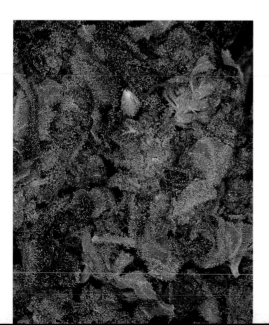

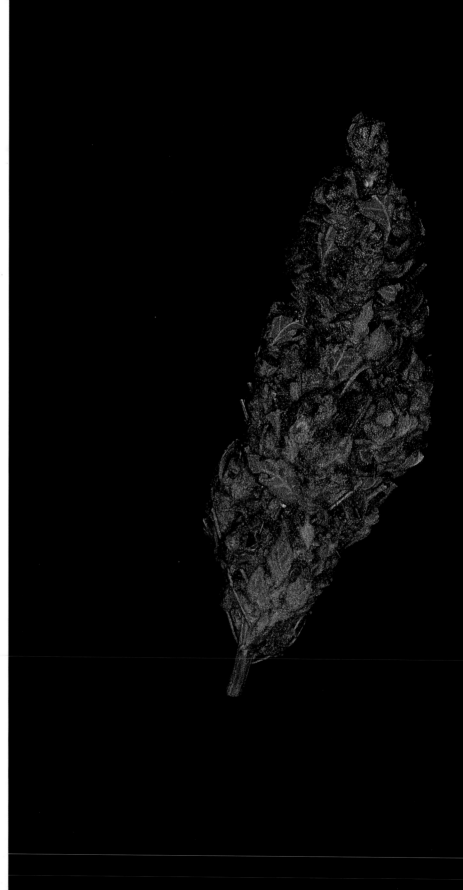

AK-47

This indica/sativa hybrid from Serious Seeds is a serious strain indeed. Winner of at least six awards, AK-47 produces extremely tight and resinous buds that give off a warm, inviting glow. The thick, expansive smoke has an interesting, woody flavor that is soft and very pleasant. The AK-47 high is very smooth and strong, yet also clear and up. The pictured sample was grown in Amsterdam using a hydroponic system.

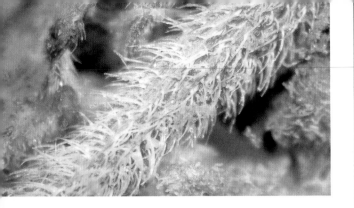

ALASKAN MATANUSKA THUNDERFUCK

This noted and gorgeous sativa strain was reportedly bred and developed in the Matanuska Valley of Alaska. The flavor of this cannabis is exquisite. It tastes like red grapes! The effects take a while to fully manifest, but the end result is a beautifully clear and euphoric high that lasts for over four hours. Very conversational, this herb reminded me of how much I prefer sativas over indicas. It should be noted that the strain Sagamartha Seeds sells as Matanuska Tundra is not related to this magnificent strain. Sagamartha's Tundra is more indica based and generic.

AMSTERDAM FLAME

Amsterdam Flame is mostly an indica, though there is definitely a sativa influence. This Paradise Seeds strain has a soft, subtle flavor that is very pleasant. The plant's aroma is also soft and sweet, with delightful, tangy overtones. The high is up for an indica, which inspired me to go to Vondelpark (a beautiful park in Amsterdam) for a more thorough testing.

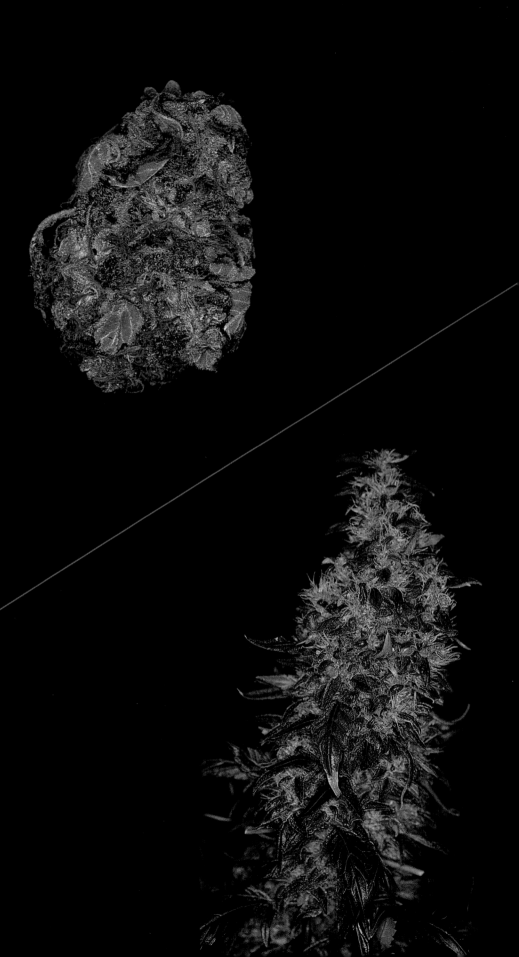

AMSTERDAM GOLD

This burly golden chunk of a bud, which is mostly a sativa, was grown indoors in Holland. The exquisite deep, penetrating smoke is slightly tainted due to a mild mold problem. Spider mites are the culprits, proving the need for a sterile growing room. Smoking mold is an extremely unhealthy practice, and should be avoided. You could easily get a lung infection, or worse. You can obtain a small, inexpensive handheld 30x microscope, making it easy to check all your buds for mold. This sample would have been amazing if not for the mold.

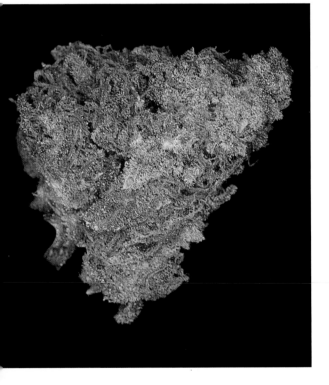

Some Things to Keep in Mind

The only way to really judge a cannabis strain's potency is to sample it. I've seen strains that had plenty of resin glands but were weak when smoked or vaporized. I've also seen strains with very few resin glands that were fantastic. The lesson learned here is that all resin glands do not contain the same amount of THC. For example, Skunk No. 1 resin glands contain much more THC than Ruderalis resin glands. To make matters even more confusing, the THC content does not necessarily provide an accurate indication of the plant's potency. I have sampled varieties that tested low for THC that were *very* psychoactive. I have also, however, smoked strains containing high quantities of THC that seemed weak and unimpressive. This could be due to the ratio of cannabidiol (CBD) and cannabinol (CBN) to THC. (CBD and CBN are accessory cannabinoids, which probably interact with THC to alter its effect, although this is not known for sure.) To repeat, sampling the herb is the only real way to know it.

ASIAN FANTASY AKA AAA

The story is as follows: Some hippies traveled in Asia during the early '70s and collected the best seeds they could find along the way. Once they arrived home in California, they grew the plants. Over the next few years, they selected plants for flavor and potency. This one was the winner. The flavor is unbelievably strong, similar to that of earthy red Lebanese hash. The ashes of this cannabis taste better than most green bud. The high is very interesting in that it never levels out—the more you smoke, the higher you get. Every toke bumps you up a notch higher. The high is powerful and lethargic, yet still inspiring—definitely nighttime bud. This plant grows in the shape of a giant upside down squid. The bud pictured at far right is an Asian hybrid grown in Maui.

Much debate exists over whether this plant is an indica or sativa. I think it is a sativa. In fact, this is undoubtedly the best sativa I've ever tried. If this strain was entered in the Cannabis Cup, it would easily win. Nothing of this quality has ever been at the Cannabis Cup. The only other strain that I've come across with as much flavor is the HP13, although they are from totally opposite sides of the spectrum. Due to its "no tolerance" character, I believe this strain has serious medicinal value and would like to see it available soon at reputable seed distributors.

Author's Note:

I understand that this variety is now extinct, due to a foolish and greedy individual who would trust no one with the strain and then lost it himself. It takes a certain amount of skill and space to keep a strain going properly, and this guy wasn't up to it. It should be noted that he was not one of the people who originally acquired the strain. He did, somehow, end up being the last person with it. There is a lesson here for all of us. If you are in possession of some amazing and rare cannabis genetics (or any heirloom plant varieties!), it is very important that they not be hoarded and that appropriate measures are taken to assure the strain's continued existence. This could mean taking the strain to the nearest Cannabis Buyers Club, or its closest equivalent. Or you might even sell clones and/or seeds of the strain to other growers and breeders.

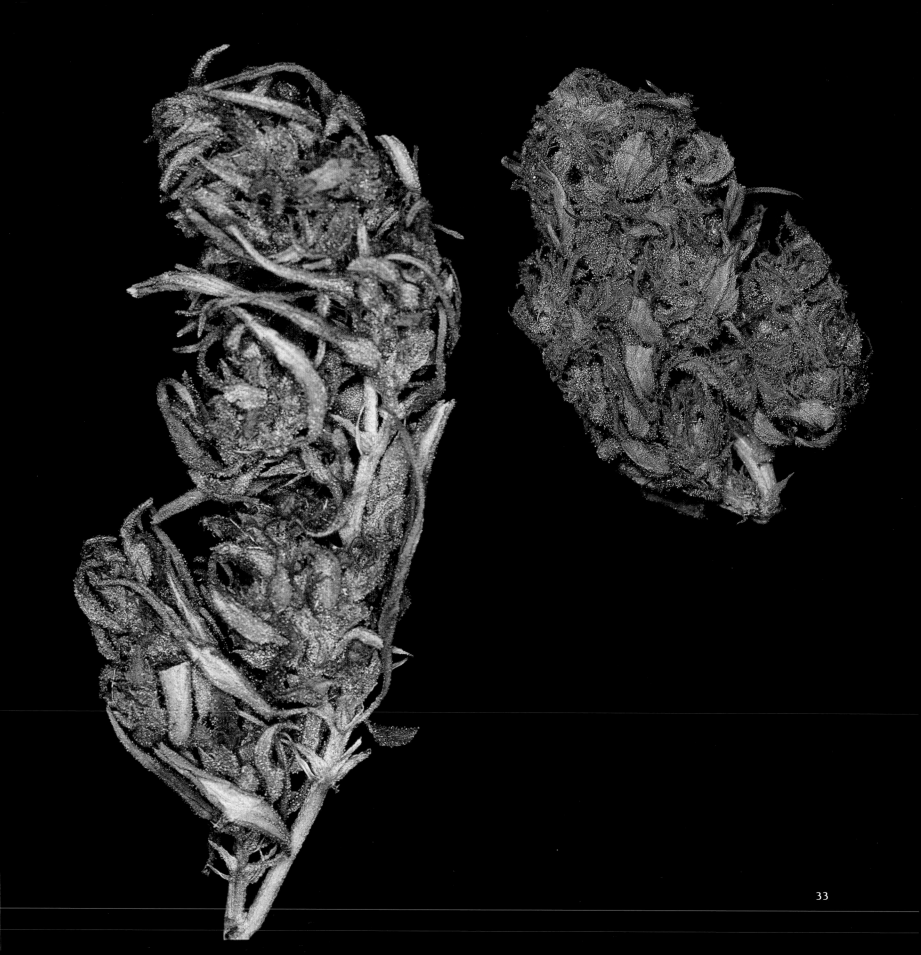

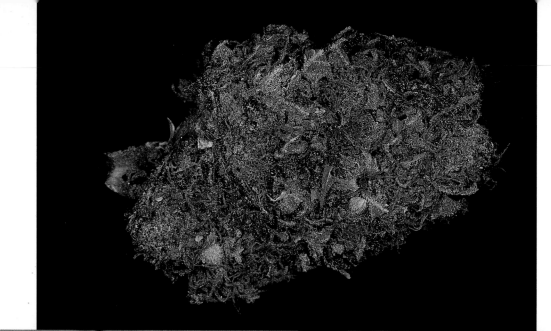

BIG BUD (EXPLODER)

Here we have the Amsterdam version of what the Dutch call "Big Bud." Yes, it is a very large bud. But it is not the Big Bud we get on the West Coast from time to time (see opposite page). This strain is not even related to the real Big Bud. It has lots of pretty red hairs, but unfortunately they aren't psychoactive. Completely boring and generic; don't waste your time. Nuff said.

BIG BUD (THE REAL ONE)

Often imitated but never duplicated, the real Big Bud is one of my personal favorites. Originally bred in the Pacific Northwest, the buds of this strain are so huge that they must be tied up or they'll fall over. Both Amsterdam and Canada have a strain called Big Bud, but they are both weak and generic in comparison to the real Big Bud. According to Amsterdam legend, Big Bud was brought to Holland as a rooted female clone. Since there are no Big Bud males, any Big Bud seeds sold had to have been crossed with a male of something else, most likely an Amsterdam Skunk. It's also possible that the Amsterdam and Canadian versions of Big Bud are not even related to the real one, and were named simply because of their large size. If the Amsterdam Big Bud is in fact related to the real Big Bud, it was crossed with a strain so weak and generic that it diluted the original Big Bud to the point of schwagginess.

As far as pedigree details go, I believe Big Bud is a Skunk selection, selected and inbred for large size and skunkiness. This is obvious when one is in the presence of this monstrously dank specimen. It smells so skunky that it simply cannot be contained; if a jar of this stuff is opened, the room immediately reeks of skunk. The flavor is extraordinary, dank, and medicinal—like taking a deep inhalation in a dungeon. The high is very powerful—some find it too strong.

I've heard of growers paying $10,000 for a single clone (which is then used as a mother), which is totally worth it considering it will produce plants over twice as weighty as most of its competitors. The $10,000 price of admission would be more than covered by the extra buds from the first harvest alone!

Solar Puffing

There is a way to ingest cannabis that is healthier, tastier, more efficient, and more ecologically sound than smoking it using a butane lighter. No, I'm not referring to vaporizing, although the effects can be pretty similar. I am speaking of solar puffing: using the sun and a magnifying lens to smoke the herb.

Here's how to do it: First, you will need a magnifying glass or lens of some sort. Larger ones work better, and plastic ones will work fine. Sit outside on a sunny day and face the sun. (You can also enjoy solar puffing indoors, provided that bright sunlight enters the room directly.) Next, put the pipe in your mouth and tilt it slightly downward. This makes it easier to focus the beam of light on the bud. Hold the lens in between the sun and the bowl, being careful not to block any of the light with the top of your hand. Start off holding the lens about six inches above the bowl. Then, adjust the height of the lens to concentrate the beam of light to a small point, where it is most intense. When you see smoke, start inhaling! That's it! You've just taken your first solar bong hit. Be careful not to stare at the brightest part of the light for too long, and also try not to burn your leg by accident!

There are many benefits to smoking the solar way. First and foremost is taste. The experience of inhaling pure ganja smoke is incredible. Solar puffing completely eliminates your exposure to the nasty butane fumes that are emitted by lighters. Flint smoke, which is highly toxic, is also avoided. Many people report that they had no idea that their herb tasted so great! The difference in flavor becomes even more evident as you reach the end of a bowl, when herb can often start tasting pretty schwaggy. And, because the bowl isn't drenched in butane, it burns clean and tasty right up to the last toke.

Once you get the hang of solar puffing, you can start experimenting with moving the beam of sunlight around the surface of the nugget. If you're able to do this at just the right speed, you can actually vaporize the bud pretty effectively. Since you're not torching the entire bowl with a huge flame, but rather vaporizing one little spot with an intense beam of light, the bowl will go around at least twice as many times as a bowl smoked with a lighter.

Wind or no wind, you'll be able to light up. And, think of the space you'll save in our landfills when you forego all those little plastic pieces of garbage (lighters) for one, nice big magnifying glass.

Finally, the last reason for solar puffing is the high. For some reason, you just get higher! It is undeniable. You may also notice that the high is much cleaner, with no head-achiness.

You might be wondering how to do solar bong hits at night. I believe the best answer is to vaporize at night, or at least use matches that are burnt past the sulfur tip. That is, unless you have a lens capable of doing lunar bong hits, in which case I'd love to see it!

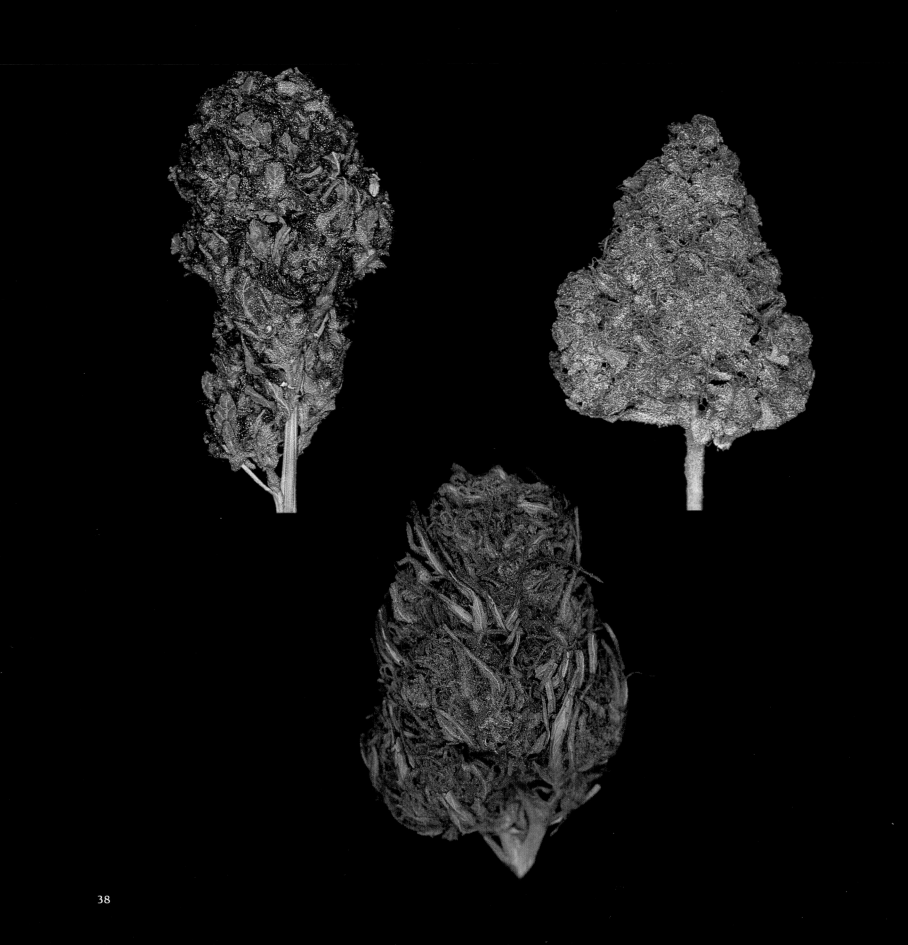

BIG BUD X HASH PLANT

This fat hybrid (opposite page, upper left and at right) was bred on the West Coast of the United States, a blend of two fine indicas. The female was a Big Bud, originally from the Pacific Northwest. This is the *real* Big Bud (see page 35) here, not an imitation Amsterdam or BC variety. The male was a juicy hash plant variety. These buds have a dank, medicinal flavor, much like taking a deep inhalation in a dungeon. This is the Big Bud's trademark flavor coming through. The high is simply mind numbing. The resin content on these plants is extremely high, a joy to behold. I would recommend a strain like this for medicinal use, as well as for cash croppers.

BIZARRE

I have only seen this strain (opposite page, upper right and below) in one place—the Dutch Flowers coffee shop in Amsterdam. They confirmed this exclusivity when I asked about it. The only genetic information I could get was that it is a five-way and it contains Citral. The thick, robust smoke produces a very clear and meditative high. The exquisite flavor is musky and pungent, with a lemony spiced aftertaste. This bud has some of the densest resin clusters I've ever seen, creating a jungle of sparkling THC bliss. This one was grown indoors in soil and it is one of my personal favorites from Amsterdam.

BLACK DOMINA

Here is another luscious offering from the Sensi Seed Bank: Black Domina, a pure indica, with a candied flavor not unlike that of hash oil mixed with baby aspirin! This mouthwatering sample (opposite page, bottom) was grown outdoors organically in Northern California. The high is quite cerebral for an indica, but it is the flavor that keeps me coming back for more.

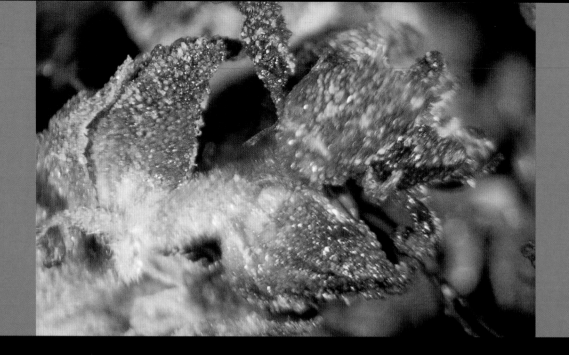

BLACK WIDOW

This bizarre strain is properly named. The bud grows in claw-shaped "pods" with eerie long black hairs. Mostly sativa, this batch was harsh due to an insufficient leaching of the chemical fertilizers that were unfortunately used for her food. Although not incredibly potent, the high made me want to go out and do something, a rare quality in most of the (indica dominated/contaminated) cannabis seen today. Interestingly, I've never seen this strain in Amsterdam, which is absolutely flooded with White Widow varieties.

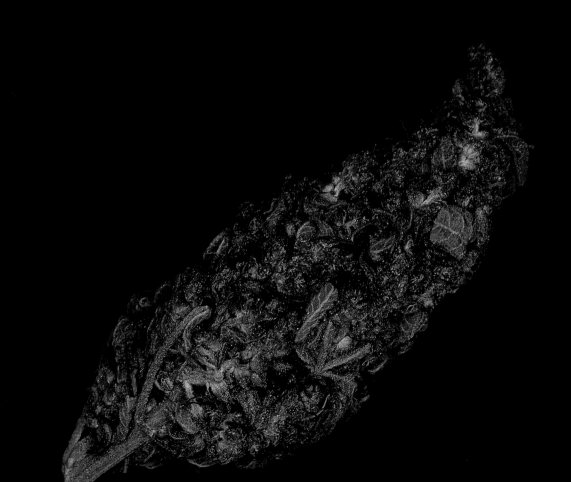

BLAZE

Here is something I found in Amsterdam that is distinctly different from other Dutch herb. This one actually reminds me of the real Big Bud (see page 35), but with slight differences. Very medicinal tasting and incredibly sticky, this one *reeks*! I couldn't roll a joint after breaking it up because my fingers were too sticky. The cluster of fat resin glands was just begging to be smoked. More info is clearly needed.

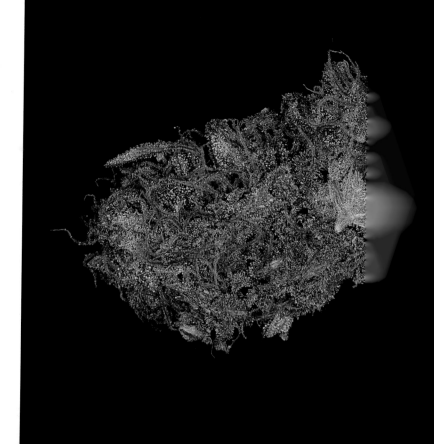

I've noticed that smoking marijuana relates to my dreamtime experiences—or lack thereof. When I first suspected that ganja smoking was either preventing dreams or clouding my memory of them, I conducted a few experiments. For three separate three-day periods, I fasted from ganja smoking. Each night of these trials, I dreamt most of the night and was able to remember and even gain insights from some of my dreams. When I returned to smoking, my dreams were either greatly diminished or completely absent. I could only remember snippets at best, and those memories quickly faded after waking up. I have since learned that I'm not alone in experiencing this side effect of marijuana; studies have shown that THC alters brain chemicals involved in sleep as well as brain wave patterns, which, in some people, can suppress REM sleep and therefore dreams. Dreams are a very special time when, I believe, the soul leaves the body to regenerate. We learn many important lessons and insights into our life in dreamtime space. For this reason, I highly recommend devoting a few days a month to not smoking.

Hydroxy tryptaphan, 5-HTP, is a sleep-enhancing agent that compensates for the reduction in serotonin levels caused by cannabis use so you can enter deep REM sleep normally. (Smokers generally have their most lucid dreams in the morning, during the last few hours of sleep, as opposed to the middle of the night as would normally be the case.) 5-HTP is a naturally derived amino acid available in pill form at most health food stores. Mugwort is an herb that also has beneficial effects on dreams when smoked. This herb helps many people restore their dreams even without giving up marijuana. B-complex vitamins can also prove beneficial, though it is not yet understood why.

BLUEBERRY

This strain is lovely, but it is not the real Blueberry (see page 44). This indica was grown indoors organically in soil, and has a pleasant, light blueberry fragrance. The high is also light and pleasant and quite mild, making this a great daytime bud.

Someone other than the breeder will often label a strain based on a perceived attribute, such as this bud being called Blueberry, when in fact, it's just a fruity Afghani with a slight blueberry flavor.

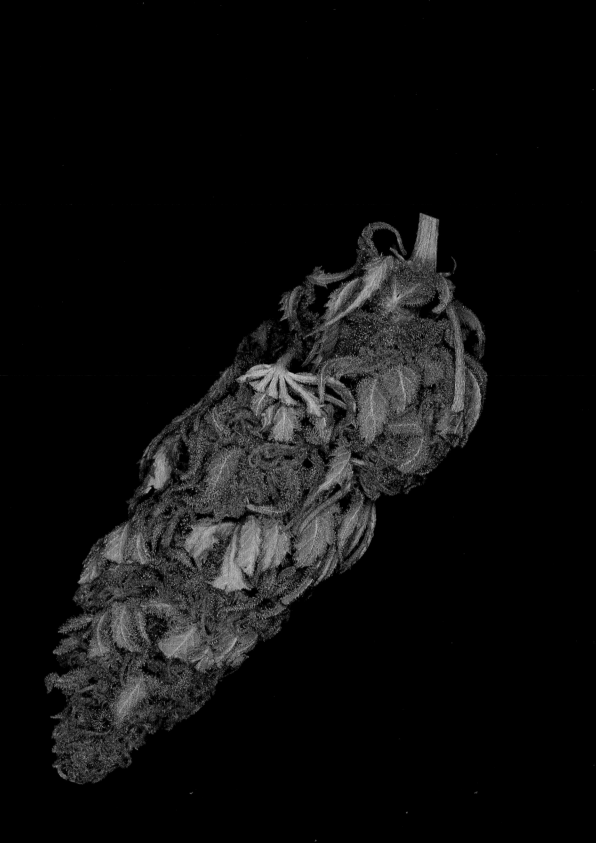

OUTDOOR
PUNA

BLUEBERRY
(THE REAL ONE!)

Ah, if only all breeders knew as much about their strains as DJ Short, the producer of Blueberry, does. The pedigree details of this Cannabis Cup 2000 winner are as follows: Three strains—Highland Thai, Purple Thai, and Afghani Indica—were used to create Blueberry (and others in DJ Short's collection).

The Highland Thai (also called Juicy Fruit Thai) was a huge, slightly hermaphroditic, slow-finishing Thai sativa plant. The Purple Thai was a first-generation cross between a Highland Oaxaca Gold (Mexican) and a Chocolate Thai. The Afghani Indica was just that—an Afghani indica. The Blueberry was discovered and stabilized from a cross between parents of a female Juicy Fruit Thai or Female Purple Thai and a male Afghani Indica. I hold a special place in my heart for the real Blueberry. The flowers are so fragrant, so . . . blue smelling. The succulent blueberry flavor stays on your tongue and your mind for hours. Highly recommended.

I do not, however, recommend buying DJ Short's strains from Sagamartha Seeds in Amsterdam; these are not authorized and are, subsequently, stolen. Dutch Passion is the only authorized distributor in Amsterdam for DJ Short's strains.

INDOOR
AMSTERDAM

ALL IMAGES: BLUEBERRY (THE REAL ONE!)

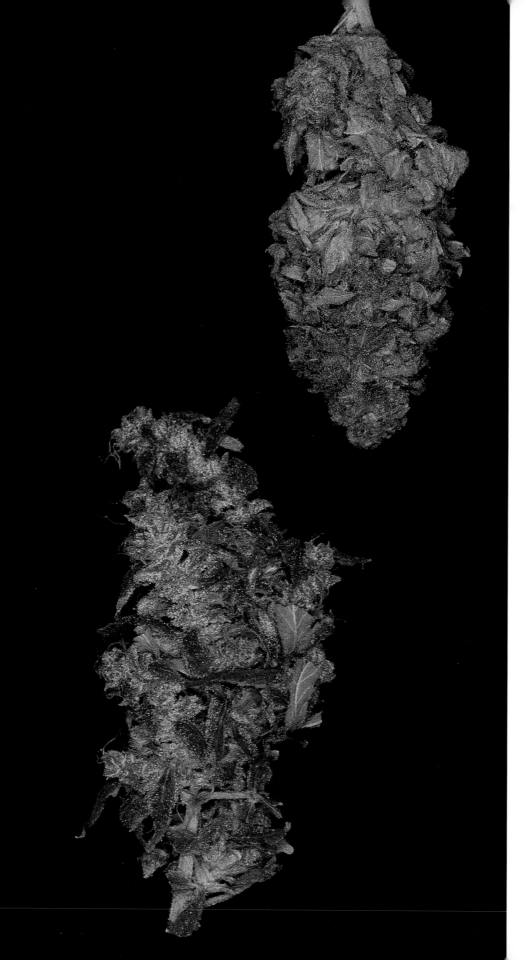

BLUE MOONSHINE

Blue Moonshine is a cousin to Blueberry. Despite what many people believe, it is not related to White Widow. Bred by DJ Short in Oregon, this strain leans toward the Juicy Fruit side of his genetic lines. The high produced is thick and warm, with soft and pleasant flavors.

BLUE VELVET

Another of DJ Short's fine Purple Thai crosses, this one balances out at 50 percent indica, 50 percent sativa. Growing trademark "foxtail" buds, the plants exhibit hues of reds and lavenders that are simply gorgeous. The high is cerebral and very clear, and it definitely does not lack potency! There is a peculiar fruitiness left on the palate that I can't put a word on, but I like it. Recommended.

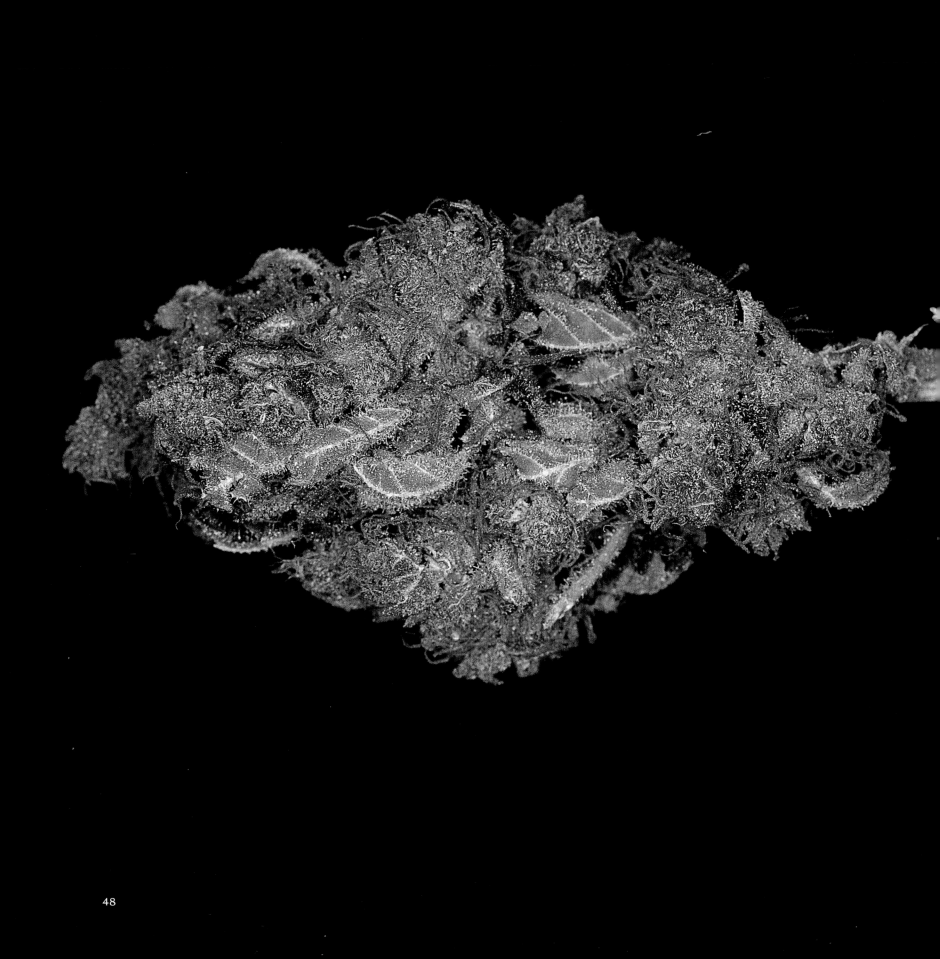

BUBBLEGUM

Bubblegum is a wonderfully fruity indica that is appearing more often these days. There are at least several different versions of Bubblegum, judging by the large diversity in samples. Reported to have originally been bred in Indiana, the strain eventually made its way to Amsterdam, where it still resides. Bubblegum and Double Bubble (opposite page)—a Bubblegum backcrossed with itself—are shown. Both were grown in Amsterdam. Lineage is as follows: Big Skunk with some NL5. The Bubblegum high is clearly uplifting and very euphoric, especially for an indica. Some plants are more bubble-gummy than others.

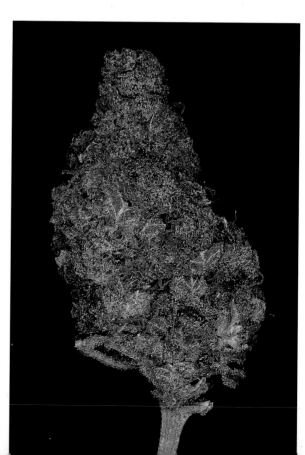

BULLRIDER

This lovely indoor strain was picked up in the San Diego, California, area, where it is one of the prominent commercially available "kind bud" strains. She has a luscious sweetness, reminiscent of a good Shiva Skunk, to which she might be related. Quite strong for commercial, this bud is absolutely fantastic in a vaporizer. The flavor is so sweet that it is almost *too* sweet! I have thus far been unable to find out any details about the strange name given to this strain.

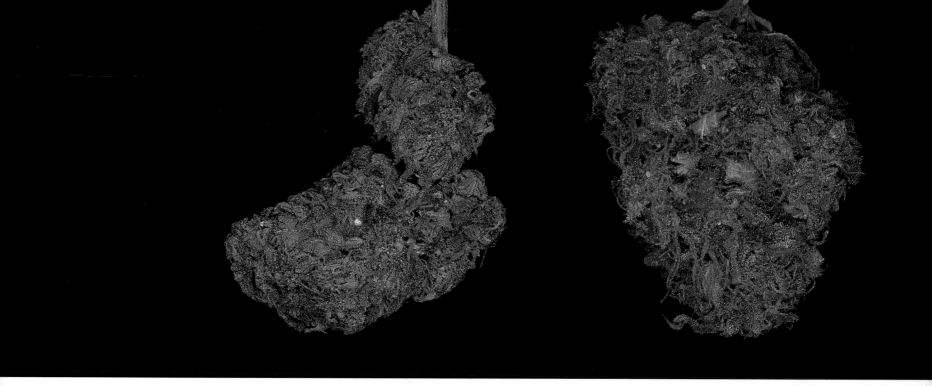

CALIFORNIA DESERT SATIVA

These mostly sativa buds were all grown outdoors organically in the deserts of Southern California. At least three different strains are in this batch, but unfortunately I couldn't get the details on lineage, as they were not known. Nevertheless, the rock-hard buds are amazing. Deep, rich flavors of total dankness with mentholated overtones are followed by a powerful, pulsating buzz.

CALIFORNIA SATIVA

This fine example of a sativa was grown organically outdoors in Southern California. This Haze-dominated strain has an incredible sweetness that seems to melt in the mouth. The high is floating and soaring, a sativa-inspired dream come true.

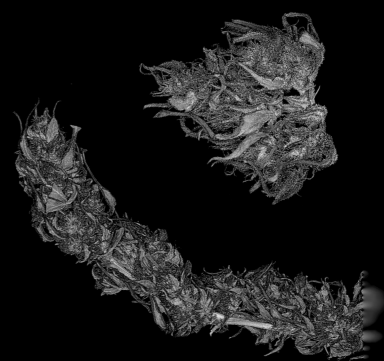

The Effects of Sativas versus Indicas

When I started smoking marijuana, I was oblivious to the different effects of each strain. I was basically just trying to catch a nice buzz and experience an alternate consciousness. As the years went by, I started paying more attention to the often subtle differences in each strain's effects. Why, I wondered, did I sometimes feel burned out and tired after smoking? Other times, admittedly more rarely, I felt uplifted and even inspired. Like many marijuana connoisseurs, I finally came to the conclusion that sativas were providing the clear and motivated high that I preferred. When I smoked a sativa, albeit a rare score, I became conversational, creative, and often very active. The body high was much more functional. The sativa's effects were cerebral, with an "up" and sometimes soaring electric buzz. On the other hand, when I smoked an indica, my eyes would become red, I would feel heavy and lethargic, and the day's events would usually proceed from a massive pig-out session to a lengthy nap. As the years progressed, I began to search for the finest sativas I could find, a hunt that became exceedingly more difficult. Due to their smaller, more manageable size and earlier harvests, most growers these days produce indicas. As a result, pure sativas have become almost impossible to find. Even with all the challenges, I still prefer a nice sativa. Don't get me wrong, sometimes I love indicas, but I prefer them late at night, when sleep is near.

In recent years, Canada, especially British Columbia, has become one of the world's largest producers of "high-grade" marijuana. There is a tremendous variety of buds coming from Canada, ranging from complete schwag to excellent. Unfortunately, most of the (indoor) buds being exported are commercially grown and mass-produced, and the quality is quite low. This is not to say that all of Canada's buds suck. Quite the contrary, the connoisseurs in Canada are puffing some seriously dank herb. Much of the outdoor herb grown is quite good, and some is awesome. Most of the stuff being exported, however, is what I call "chemmy indo no love bud." To the untrained eye and lungs, these buds look great, and so many people therefore believe they are great. To the trained eye and lungs, however, a different story unfolds. Most of the exported indoor BC has not been properly flushed before harvest, which results in the smoking of fertilizer salts. This is a wake-up call to British Columbia commercial growers—stop sending the schwag! And for Goddess's sake, please leach out the chemicals before harvest!

BC INDOOR

At right are some of the best BC buds I've come across yet, after having turned down numerous batches of complete schwag! From over seventy BC strains photographed and sampled while creating this book, only the few pictured were worthwhile. The quality of BC buds exported to America is just terrible. I often hear British Columbia folks brag about how the best buds in the world are coming from their locale. Well, this may be true, but they're certainly not sending any down to the States!

BC OUTDOOR

This chunky bud (opposite page, bottom) was grown outdoors in British Columbia. I was unable to get specific info on the genetics; however, I can say that this bud is better than over 99 percent of the indoor BC buds I've come across. Slightly reminiscent of California outdoor marijuana, the smoke is sweet and smooth, the high clear and mild. This is a welcome change from the usual indoor BC schwag. At immediate right, is another BC outdoor-grown bud, Texada Timewarp, and is probably the best BC-grown bud I've tried. Its flavor is tangy and delicious, and its high, though quite strong, was functional and plausible for daytime.

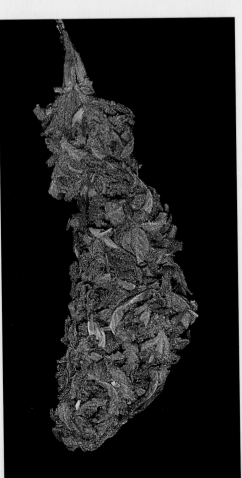

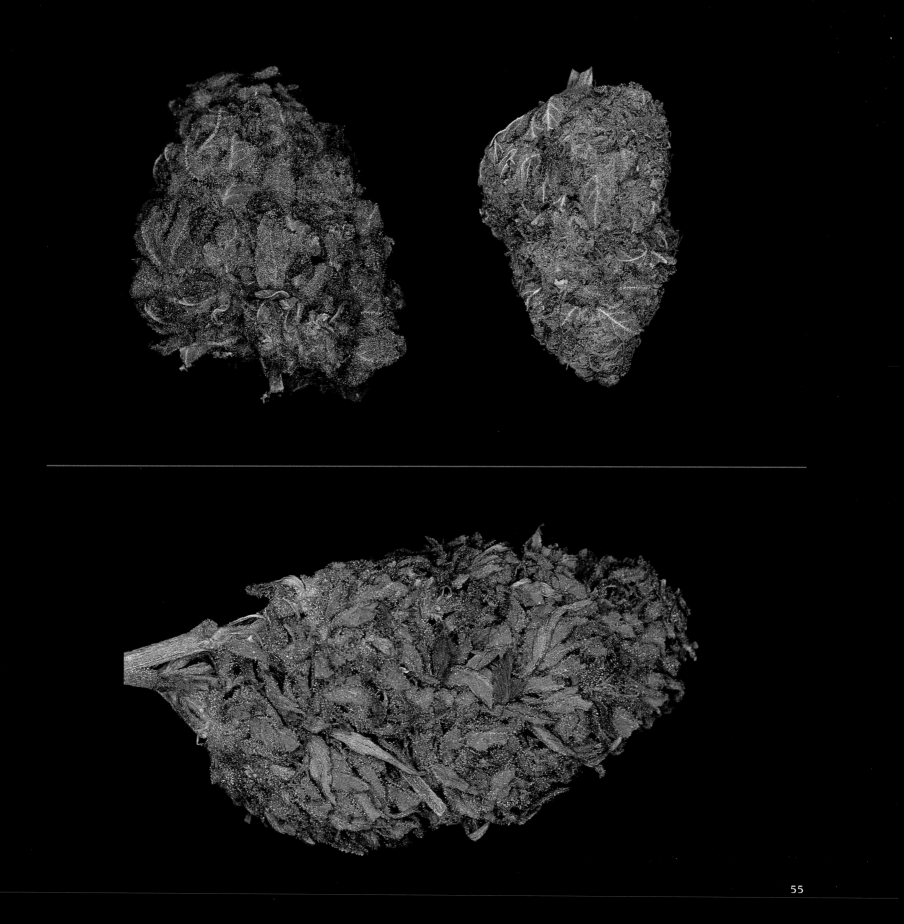

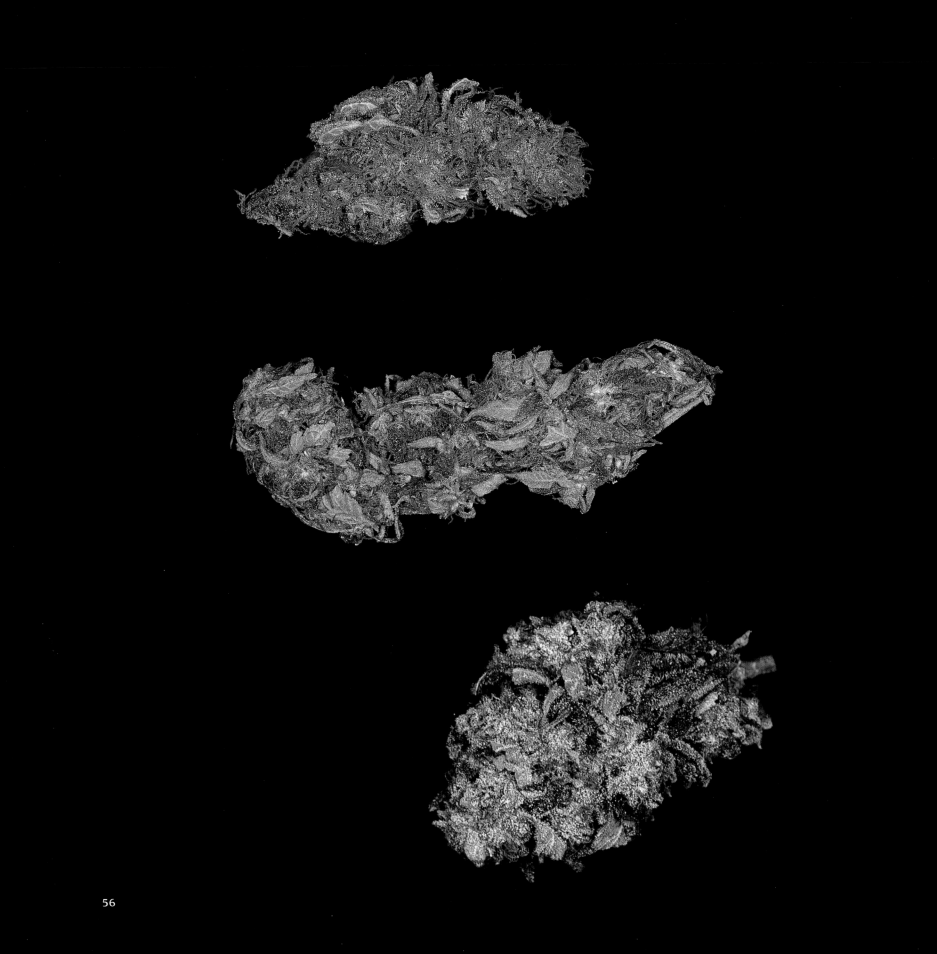

BIG FATTY

Scored and photographed in British Columbia, Big Fatty (opposite page, top) is actually a T. H. Seeds strain coming out of Amsterdam. The genetic makeup is something like this: Northern Lights x Big Bud x Northern Lights x Northern Lights—a double-back cross. The buds are sweet and a little musty, and the high is about average for an indica.

IGGY (BC)

This was supposed to be a twenty-year-old Canadian strain (opposite page, middle). Seemed pretty schwaggy to me. The taste and high were both unmemorable.

ROMULAN

Grown indoors and (supposedly) originating in British Columbia, Romulan (opposite page, bottom and this page, right) is definitely some sort of (Californian) Haze hybrid. These buds are absolutely delicious, with a spicy flavor and a warped psychedelic high. Smoke enough of this and you just might Kling-on to your couch all day! How come Canadians never send this stuff down to America, eh? (Microphotography of Romulan bud shown at upper right.)

57

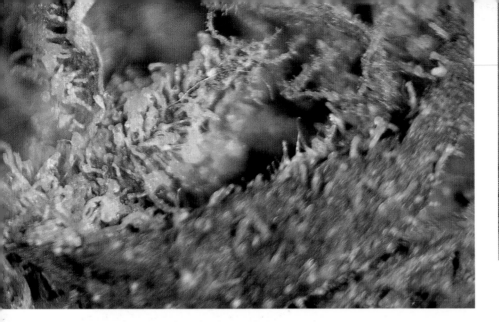

CAT PISS

These exotic buds smell great individually, but a few ounces reek like cat piss, hence the name. The flavor is very distinctive: thick and heavy, with a musky attribute. The high is pulsating and almost overpowering; it gave me the wobbles. Notice the "roots" of the resin glands growing through the leaflet surface shown via microphotography on the bud at left. I haven't seen this anywhere else. This creepy sativa (opposite page, top) was grown hydroponically indoors in California. It's very antimotivational, but great for sitting on the couch and staring into space.

CHERRY BOMB

Shown on the opposite page, bottom, is a mostly sativa plant with a zesty, thick cherry flavor not unlike that of children's cough medicine. Grown indoors in soil, this Southern Californian strain produces a mild buzz of a relatively clear nature.

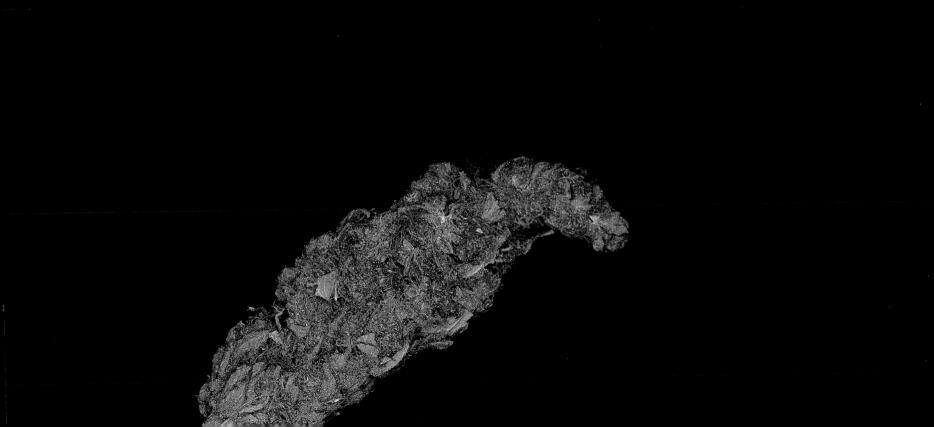

CHRONIC

Chronic is an offering from the small but impressive collection of Serious Seeds. She's mostly an indica, but there's definitely a sativa influence in there. Reportedly a Northern Lights crossed with Afghani, Chronic has a peculiar flavor that reminds me of celery. At the same time, it's pungent and somewhat musty. This one's a real heavy yielder and comes recommended for cash croppers who desire something more interesting than what they currently grow.

CITRAL

This scrumptious nugget (right) is of the Citral variety (also known as Chitral), a strain originating in Pakistan. Light yet distinctive, the buds have a wonderful lemon fragrance and flavor. There is a touch of spiciness, making the overall smoking experience quite delicious. Citral strains are not usually known for strong potency; however, they still produce a wonderful clear high. This is recommended for people who like the lighter stuff.

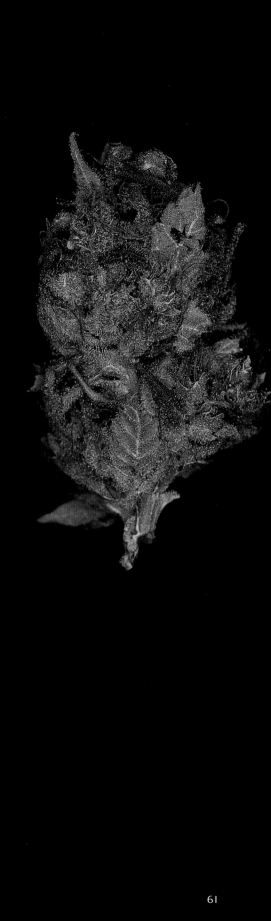

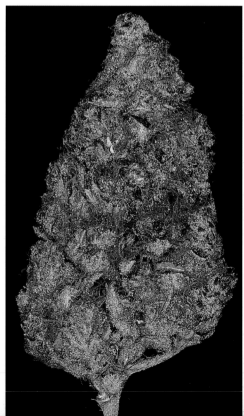

CRISTALLICA

Finally, a strain for metal heads! Cristallica is a 100 percent indica offered by Greenhouse Seed Company. The bud (left) has a pungent sublimeness, with a slight celery-flavored aftertaste. As far as pedigree details go, she's a three-way hybrid containing an Indian and two Brazilian strains. The high is strong and cloudy.

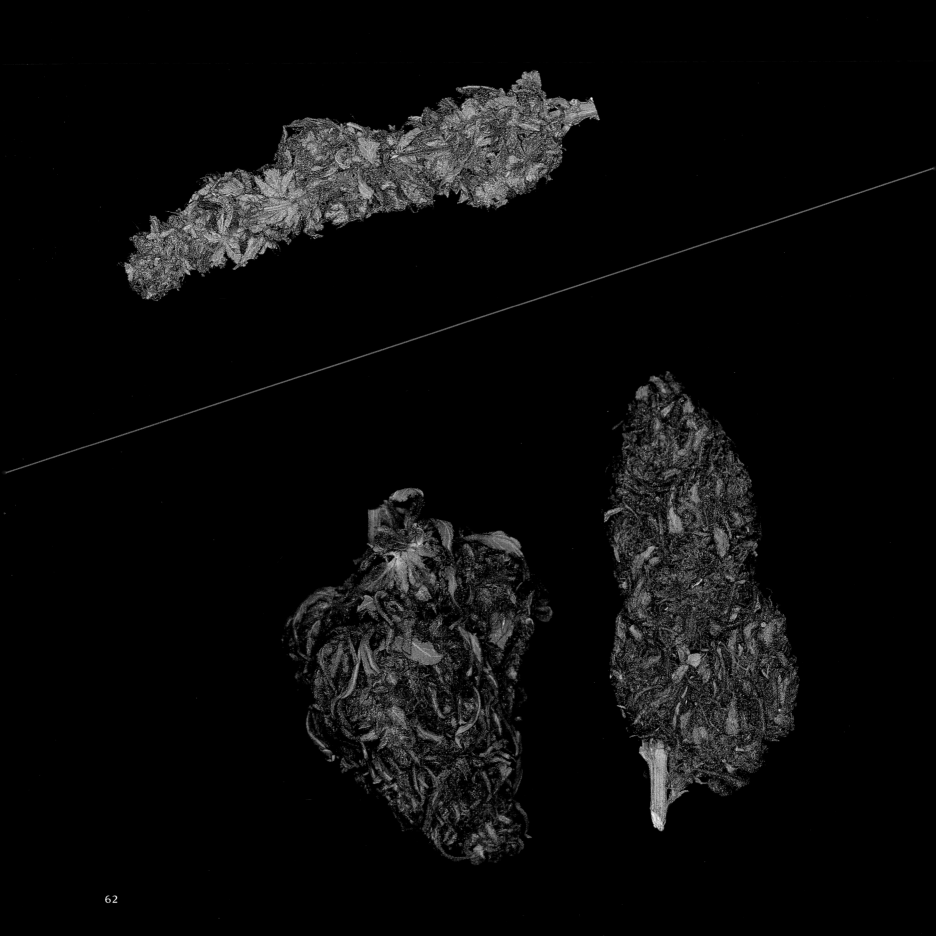

CRYSTAL LIMIT

Yet another Widow cross, this one (opposite page, top) blends rather nicely with a Haze father. Highly crystallized, with a soft and spicy smoke, Crystal Limit leans toward the maternal Widow (indica) side, evident by its narcotic-feeling buzz.

DESERT OUTDOOR ORGANIC

These delicious nuggets (opposite page, bottom) were grown outdoors organically in a desert in Southern California. They have a rich, slightly menthol fruity smell, but not much flavor. Overall, the smoke is incredibly smooth, and the high is warm and meditative. Shown fresh (opposite page, lower left) and a year old (opposite page, lower right), these buds were stored in jars in a dark place. Unfortunately, no refrigeration was used, and the deterioration is quite noticeable. The moral here is: If you can't store your buds in a cold and dry environment such as a refrigerator, smoke it within a couple of months.

Too Much of a Good Thing?

If your body needs a rest from ganja smoking, the best thing you can do is just that—give it a rest. A month- or two-month-long ganja fast won't kill you, I promise! Here are some other options that, in my experience, help get the body back up to speed.

CALAMUS ROOT TEA—Ayurvedic healers have used this medicinal root for thousands of years. It has a wonderful effect on the liver; it purges THC like nothing else can, thereby giving the liver a much-needed rest. Calamus root can be purchased in any good Chinese herb store. Boil the chopped-up root in a ceramic pot for thirty to forty-five minutes and drink the tea several times a day.

BASIL PILLS—Basil is wonderful for the lungs, and any heavy smoker would be well advised to take it every day. Blessings in a Bottle makes high-quality organic basil pills, but any source—especially fresh basil—will do.

FRESH GINGER AND LEMON TEA—This is a fantastic cleanser for the liver and kidneys. Licorice works nicely to sweeten and balance the blend.

COLTSFOOT AND MULLEIN—Smoked or preferably vaporized, these herbs, which can be found in any good herb or health food store, are very healing for the lungs.

ACUPUNCTURE—This ancient Chinese healing art can provide tremendous benefits to heavy smokers, or anyone else for that matter. By using tiny needles, an acupuncturist can stimulate energy in weakened organs, such as the lungs or liver, thus helping them heal.

VAPORIZATION—Switch to vaporization, discussed on pages 124–125.

MINT AND LICORICE ROOT—Vaporizing cannabis mixed with mint and licorice root has a very nice effect.

DIAMOND LEAF

This hydroponically grown indica is average in all respects. Interestingly, the leaves of this strain grow in a diamond shape. The flavor is slightly sweet and very boring, and the effects are also uninteresting. She was grown indoors in Amsterdam.

DIESEL

An outstanding New York City strain, Diesel is a direct descendant of the famous Chem strain. This hydro bud has a spiciness that is absolutely sublime, but it is not the familiar Haze spiciness. This one is more candied tasting, with an almost petrol tinge. Having never experienced this flavor before, I immediately fell in love with it. Unheard of in Amsterdam, Diesel would be welcome in my bubbler any time. The heavy, penetrating indica buzz made me wobbly and seems to have profound effects on gravity.

DOC KEVORKIAN

This one made me wish I were dead. Nuff said.

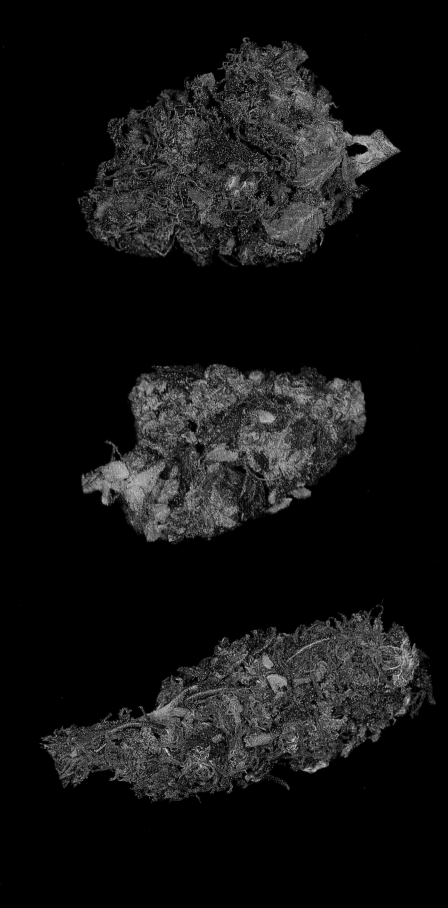

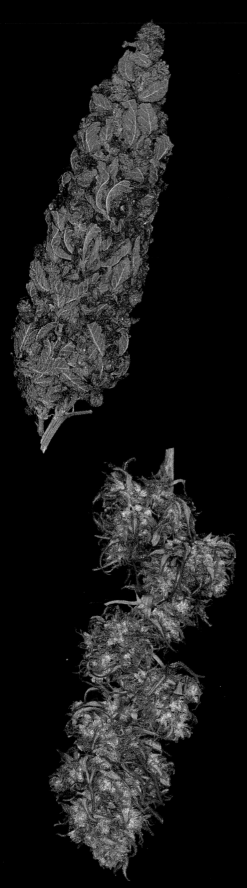

DURBAN POISON

This burly pure sativa originates in South Africa. These plants finish very early and love lots of sunlight. The bud shown on the opposite page, upper right, was grown indoors organically in soil. Also shown are a Maui outdoor version (opposite page, lower right), which was much more psychoactive; and a Maui greenhouse version (opposite page, left), which didn't seem quite as potent as the outdoor bud. Durban's high is very energetic; you can still function after smoking it, though it is quite strong. The taste is rich and satisfying, with a deep perfumy anise scent. Durbans have been heavily bred since the '70s; however, it is one of the only pure sativas left.

DURBAN POISON X MATANUSKA THUNDERFUCK

Alaska meets Africa. This fluorescent bud just about glows in the dark. By crossing two amazing sativas, this breeder produced a phenomenal strain. Deep, perfume-flavored smoke brought me to a soaring clean high that never seemed to fade. Eventually, reentry to reality is smooth and gentle. I found this specimen in Oregon, a leader in superior cannabis strains. It was grown indoors organically in soil.

DUTCH DRAGON

This highly resinous plant is mostly a sativa, and it is part of the Paradise Seeds collection in Amsterdam. Paradise strains are just now starting to pop up in Amsterdam coffee shops, a welcome addition in my opinion. The high is extremely strong, yet still functional.

EARLY DURBAN

This frosted beauty is a Durban hybrid available from The Flying Dutchmen seed company. She really oozes a lot of resin, and the aroma is unmistakably Durban, but with a twist. I felt intoxicated just from smelling this stunning plant. The high also leans toward the sativa side, with clear cerebral action. There is, however, some indica in there, so this one can also be pretty physical at times.

EARLY PEARL

These plants were grown from Sensi Seeds' Early Pearl selection. Early Pearl is a crossing of Pollyanna, a sativa from the '70s, and Early Girl, a cross of Afghani and Mexican sativa. Highly mold resistant, Early Pearl finishes early and is known to handle pretty harsh conditions outdoors, making her highly desirable to some. The high is clear and mild, but sort of trippy as well. They were grown outdoors in Maui, where they matured from seed to harvest in only fifty-nine days.

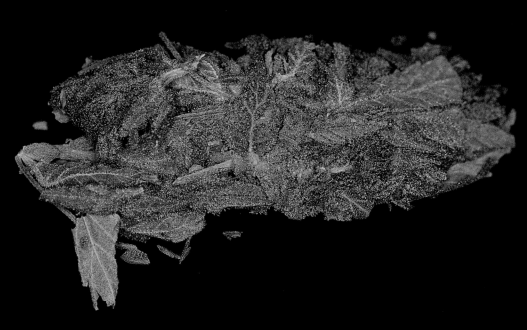

FLO

Flo is an early maturing 60 percent sativa/40 percent indica cross that produces the most motivational high I've ever experienced. After smoking some Flo, I couldn't sit around. I had to get up and do something. What a wonderful quality for a strain to possess. The flavor is also quite distinctive; similar to a juicy piece of Royal Nepalese hashish, it is full bodied, thick, and ambrosial. Leaning toward the Purple Thai end of DJ Short's collection, I recommend it highly.

FOUR-WAY

This is a four-way hybrid (below, left) of some of Amsterdam's most common indoor strains: Afghani, Ruderalis, Northern Lights, and Skunk No.1. Because of the large amount of genetic possibilities inherent with any multiple hybrid, expect lots of variety in this strain. The flavor is the standard Amsterdam sweetness, which is boring in my opinion. The high is also average at best, in every respect.

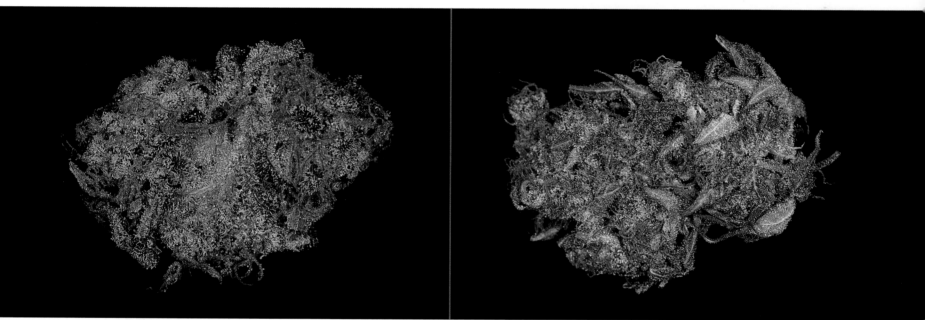

4077 MED LEAF

Here's a strain (above, right) that I've only seen at The Grey Area coffee shop in Amsterdam. I assume the name is some sort of a *M.A.S.H.* reference. This incredibly resinous strain has a medicinal flavor not unlike that of the real Big Bud. The high is thick and heavy, a hint of the indica background lurking. I recommend trying some of this on a visit to the 'Dam. It reminds me of good American herb, not surprising since the shop is run by Americans.

GAK

Gak is a Kush hybrid strain grown indoors in the coastal area of Southern California. The high is thick and heavy, and is felt mostly in the head.

GREAT WHITE SHARK

Super Skunk and White Widow were crossed to create this Greenhouse Seed Company strain. It's just another reshuffling of tired old Amsterdam strains. The high of this particular batch was unimpressive.

G-13

Some say this strain comes from a clone stolen from the U.S. Government Marijuana Research Facility, located in Mississippi. Others say this is untrue, that the stuff the government grows is crap. I agree with the latter. Two different G-13s are shown, one from Trichome Technologies, tested at a whopping 27.2 percent THC (right), and one picked up in San Diego (above). Both are incredibly strong. Not much flavor, but hey, these babies were bred for THC, not flavor! If G-13 were in fact a stolen clone, then two different ones would not exist, unless one of the clones was bred with something different. Go figure.

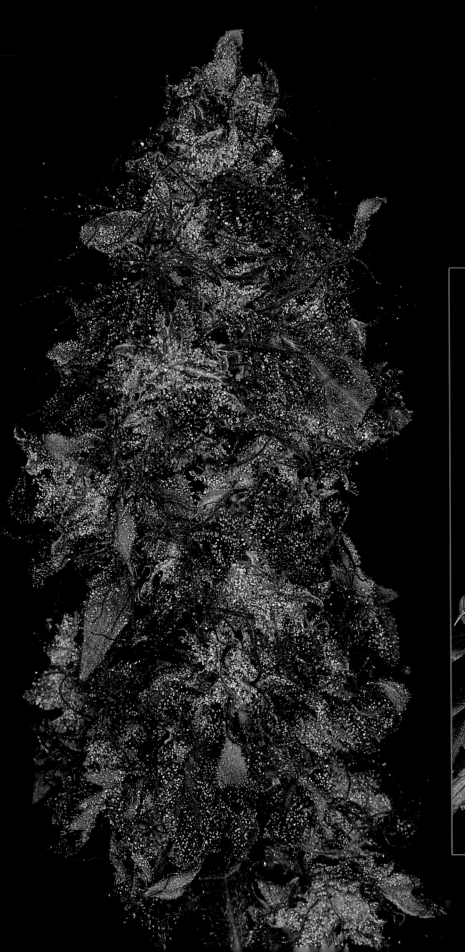

HP13
MAUI INDOOR

HASH PLANT

This hydroponically grown bud (opposite page, left) is a pure indica from Afghanistan. Massive resin output makes it great for making hash, which, not coincidentally, is what it was originally bred for. This strain has a strong narcotic high, complete with a red-eyed fog to drift around in. There are many different versions of Hash Plant, or HP, and they range from mediocre to outrageous. This Californian-grown batch was raised in a closet with a heat problem, so the buds stretched out a little. Despite the heat irregularity, this one rates excellent and is recommended for any indica lover.

HP13

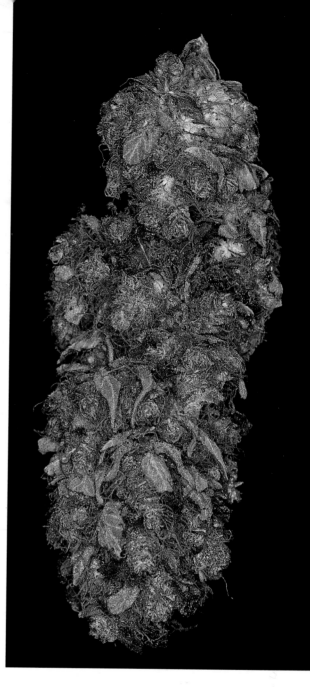

This strain is called HP13, or Hash Plant #13. The inner circle of pot snobs lucky enough to have access to it sometimes lovingly refer to it simply as "P." This pure indica strain originated in Afghanistan, and was surely inbred for generations by a proud family line of Afghanis in some remote valley of the Pakistani/Afghani mountain range. Then in the '70s, as more and more westerners traveled the infamous hippy hashish trail, some of this magical gene pool was brought to America in the form of seeds. The strain stayed in California for a while, and eventually made its way to New York City of all places, where it is commonly sold for over twice the cost of gold ($8,000 a pound and up)! At right is a NYC version. Two things are notable about this strain of marijuana: the flavor, and the psychological effects it has on people—*not* necessarily from smoking it. HP13 has the most complex flavor I have ever experienced, and I'm not limiting that statement to just ganja. This herb tastes so incredible it could easily be described as erotic. New flavors visit the taste buds minutes after the smoke is exhaled; the range of flavors is truly impressive. This diverse flavor can hardly be put to words, but I'll try. Skunky, garlicky, salty, spicy, hashy, and the list goes on. All it takes is one toke, and most pot smokers become instant P-heads. Many "friendships" have been made and lost over this strain, sometimes over and over again. I am not proud to admit that I nearly lost a close friend trying to get a quarter ounce. I also lament breaking, for the first time ever, my rule of never paying more than $100 for a quarter. I paid $115, which was actually considered a "bro deal," and in all honesty, it was totally worth it. The ashes of this bud taste better than the green hits of most other "kind" bud. It's so strong that many experienced smokers can't handle it, and have paranoid or nauseous reactions. A sizeable amount of this magical herb was brought to the Cannabis Cup in '94, but it was so good that certain organizers, who shall remain nameless, hoarded it and, therefore, it never made it to the judges. This definitely falls into the "psychological effects" category.

HP13 pros and cons: The pros, everybody wants to be your friend; the cons, all other pot tastes like hay now.

HASH PLANT #14

This Hash Plant is a bit of an enigma; it's totally different from HP13, or any other Hash Plant for that matter. Photographed at the Sensi Seed Bank breeding facility in Holland, this hydroponically grown strain appears to have a very sativa-dominated growth pattern, resembling Jack Herer. I was assured, however, by Alan Dronkers that it was in fact a pure indica. When I tried some of this spectacular herb, I was convinced. The smoke, although not extremely flavorful, has that familiar indica pungency. Its narcotic high truly convinced me. Within minutes, my eyes were red and I seemed to be getting heavier.

Organic versus Hydro versus Bio

There has been much recent debate over different styles of marijuana growing, and confusion lingers for many people. Here are some important points to understand about marijuana growing styles. "Organic" means that no chemicals are used in any part of the growing process. Most often, organic growing is done in soil, whether indoor or outdoor. "Hydro," or hydroponic growing, means that no soil is used. Many other planting mediums are available, such as rockwool, coconut husks, clay pellets, sand, and even air. Contrary to many people's assumption (based on the root "hydro"), water is not used as a medium in hydroponic growing; it is only used periodically, as with any growing method, to hydrate the plant.

Most hydroponic growers use synthetic fertilizers, and the finished product's quality suffers as a result. You can grow organic hydroponics by using liquid organic nutrients. Liquefied nutrients flow easily through most hydroponic systems. Unfortunately, not many people are doing this, probably because they fear their yield will suffer if they stop pumping their plants up with chemicals. This is simply not the case. When done properly, organics are just as heavy yielding, and sometimes heavier, than hydroponics.

Organic growing has allowed this AK-47 bud to more fully express its maximum overall potential.

"Bio," a term mostly heard in Europe, means the plant was grown in soil. It does not mean organic—in fact, much of what is called bio is not organically grown.

In my observation, soil-grown organics are the *only* way to go. For one thing, the smoke is much tastier. Subtle flavors are easily discerned, flavors that are completely missed when the sample is grown hydroponically and/or chemically. I have taken two buds from the same strain, one grown organically in soil and the other grown hydroponically, and smoked them side by side for comparison purposes. There was no comparison. The organic bud had a multitude of flavors, one appearing after another on my delighted palate. I could even pick up the earthy flavor of the soil in which it was grown. The bud burned properly down to the last hit, leaving a clean gray ash. The hydro bud tasted good on the first hit, though the flavor was not complex like the organic one. It was a straightforward sweetness, which was boring compared to the robust and varied flavors of the organic sample. Instead of picking up the earthy flavor of soil, I was left with a chemically burnt flavor in my mouth. To make matters worse, the bud did not burn well and slowly transformed into a black chunk of carbon-like crud. Also, most hydro bud eventually leaves me with a headache, which rarely happens when I smoke organic. Now I will only smoke organic herb. (Though I do make an exception occasionally....)

Most of these delectable nuggets were grown outdoors organically on the Big Island of Hawaii. Several legendary Hawaiian strains—mostly sativas and all of amazing quality—are pictured. Big Island buds are uniquely different from those from Maui, or anywhere else for that matter. Typically, they are small (under three inches) and dense with lots of big fat bracts. They almost always pack a wallop of a stone, but the flavors are really where it's at. Many heavenly flavors that I've not tasted elsewhere exist within the Big Island cannabis gene pool. The Puna Budda is still flowing these days, much like the still-flowing Kilauea volcano.

BLUE BURMESE

With genetics from the jungles of Burma, this mostly indica is too heavy for most smokers. Definitely a nighttime bud.

HAWAIIAN/SAN DIEGO

Pure joy—that is what these buds represent (opposite page). The strain comes from Hawaii; however, these buds were grown in San Diego, California. This delicious outdoor-grown herb with a peculiar fruity taste and smell, is a tangy and tropical delight with a definite Haze influence. The high is very giggly and heavy, with extreme cases of the munchies. Although the legendary quality of Hawaiian marijuana is due more to the outstanding tropical growing conditions in the islands than the actual strain, this San Diego–grown Hawaiian definitely captures some of the mellow aloha vibe. Also pictured (opposite page, top, center) is another Hawaiian strain grown in California. Once again, very nice, but it's not quite the same as da island–grown kine.

BLUE BURMESE

OREGON BIG BUD

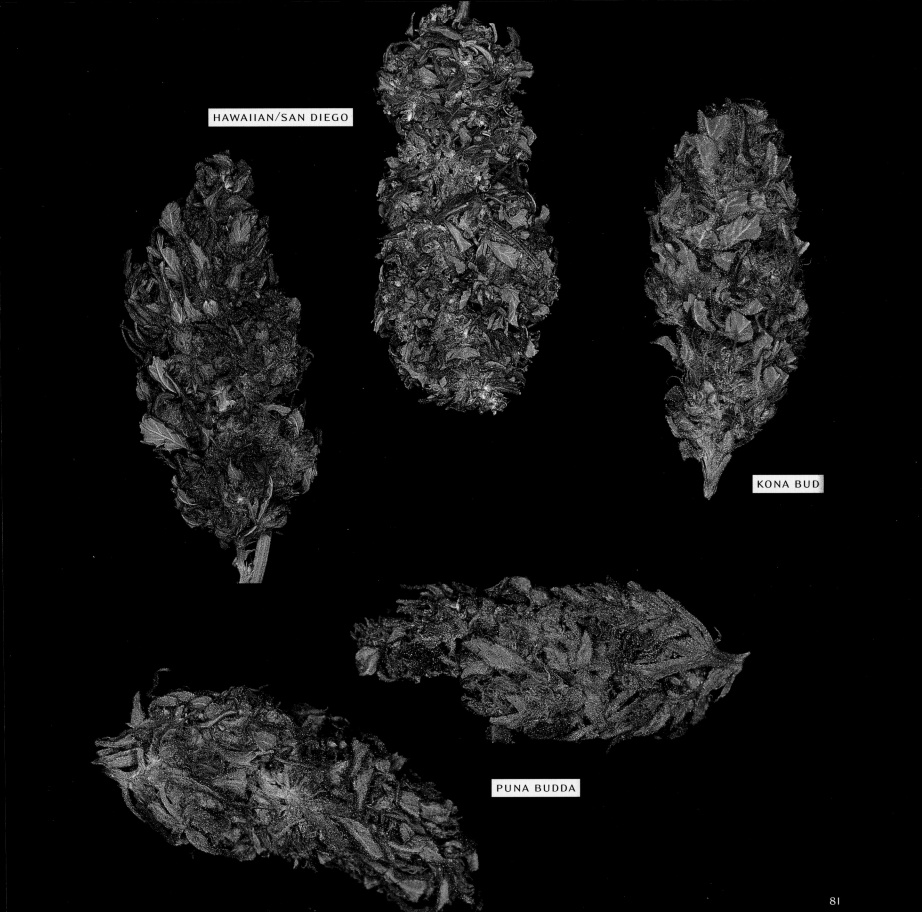

HAWAIIAN/SAN DIEGO

KONA BUD

PUNA BUDDA

REDWAY REDEYE

RUDERALIS X
STRAWBERRY WEB

STRAWBERRY WEB

An old Hawaiian strain—spicy, tropical, fruity, yummy! This strain grows with webbed leaves.

SWAHILI

A pure South African sativa (below)—has a heavenly, soft, ambrosial smoke. It's strong yet clear! These buds consist almost entirely of bracts—leaflet surfaces with the highest concentration of resin glands.

THAI

WAIILE BUD

HAWAIIAN X PENNSYLVANIA PURPLE (NEW YORK)

This beautiful bud (opposite page, lower left) was grown outdoors in New York State. A Hawaiian sativa strain was crossed with a Pennsylvanian Purple strain to create this yummy hybrid. The buds have a deep, smooth, and rich flavor that is quite subtle at first. Upon exhalation, the aftertaste begins forming—a balmy fruitiness reminding me of lemons. The high is also nice, a bit floaty at times, but nothing extraordinary.

HAZE

Haze is a four-way super-sativa consisting of Colombian, Mexican, Thai, and South Indian strains. The herb (opposite page, upper left) must be tasted to be believed. The flavor is extremely strong and spicy. The high is clear, energetic, and most of all, *strong!* Haze is one of the few strains of the '70s that still survives, primarily because it made it to Amsterdam. Originally bred in Santa Cruz, California, a more Colombian version of Haze ended up in Amsterdam. While it's very easy to find Haze in Amsterdam, you will not find ı in its pure form. The people who have access to real Haze use it for breeding purposes only. If they were to grow it pure, it would harvest very little and take forever. Luckily, even 50 percent Haze is incredible! The bud pictured is 50 percent Haze, 50 percent Skunk (probably) and is about as close to pure Haze as can be found nowadays.

HAZE X SKUNK

Two classic sativas meet head on in this hybrid. In the bud pictured at upper right, Haze was the mother and Skunk was the father. In the bud pictured at lower right, Skunk was the mother and Haze was the father. As you can see, they are quite different. Unfortunately, they are both Amsterdam grown commercial schwag, in my opinion, and both left me craving some dank bud. It is important to note that if either of these strains was grown with love, organically, they would have been fantastic. This is not just hippie lore I'm speaking of here—it's been scientifically proven. In *Secret Life of Plants,* by Tompkins and Bird, experiments are discussed wherein two identical gardens are planted next to each other; one garden has a group of people that sits around the plants and, well, loves the plants several times per day. The other garden receives identical treatment, except for the love sessions. The "loved" garden had substantially greater harvest size, tastier veggies, and even higher nutritional content! Love is the *best* fertilizer!

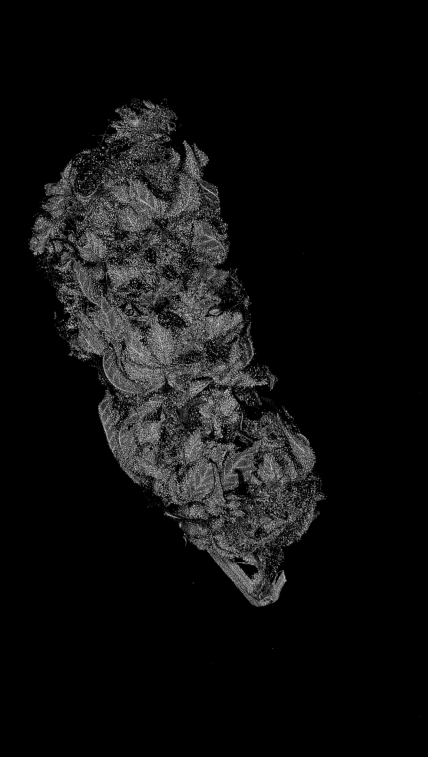

HEROAUNA

This shockingly strong indica is so potent that most people simply should not smoke it. After vaporizing three hits, I fully understood the strain's given name. The flavor, best appreciated in a vaporizer, is candied and hashy, though not overwhelming. The high (or low) is what is noteworthy. I have a *very* high tolerance and it still made me stutter; I was unstable—bumping into things—at times, nauseous, and even slightly paranoid. Imagine what it would do to a lightweight. I would estimate this bud at 25 percent THC at least, probably more. It seems much stronger than G-13. In fact, it seems stronger than 50 percent THC hash that I have smoked. A nap was inevitable, the kind of nap when you wake up the next day with your eyes still glued shut and a hang-over! The lineage is Northern Lights x Hash Plant, but these genetics are from the "old-school"—not exactly the same as what you would get in Amsterdam these days. Recommended for lovemaking, appetite stimulation, inducing sleep, or if you just like knockout indicas. Hope you don't have any plans for the rest of the day!

HIMALAYAN GOLD

This Greenhouse Seed Company offering is a delightful cross of Nepali, Indian, and Vietnamese strains. The buds have a succulent fruitiness, with a tang. The high is clear and thorough, a sign of the sativa-based breeding material used.

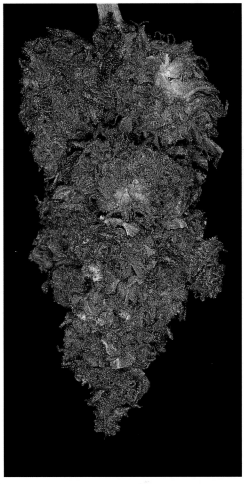

HINDU KUSH

With its origins in the foothills of the Hindu Kush mountain range in Afghanistan, this extremely stinky indica exists in many different forms around the world. Generally, Kush plants are short, stocky, early maturing, and potent. As true-breeding stable strains, they make wonderful parental material for breeding purposes. Originally used for making hash, today these strains have found their way into just about everything. Look for the typical wide-bladed indica leaves and the knockout stone. Three different versions are pictured: a California indoor organic soil-grown Kush (right), a hydroponically grown indoor BC Kush (opposite page, upper right), and an Amsterdam hydro Kush (opposite page, upper left). The organic one, quite predictably, is by far the best, with subtle grape-like tones of earthy flavor dancing on the taste buds.

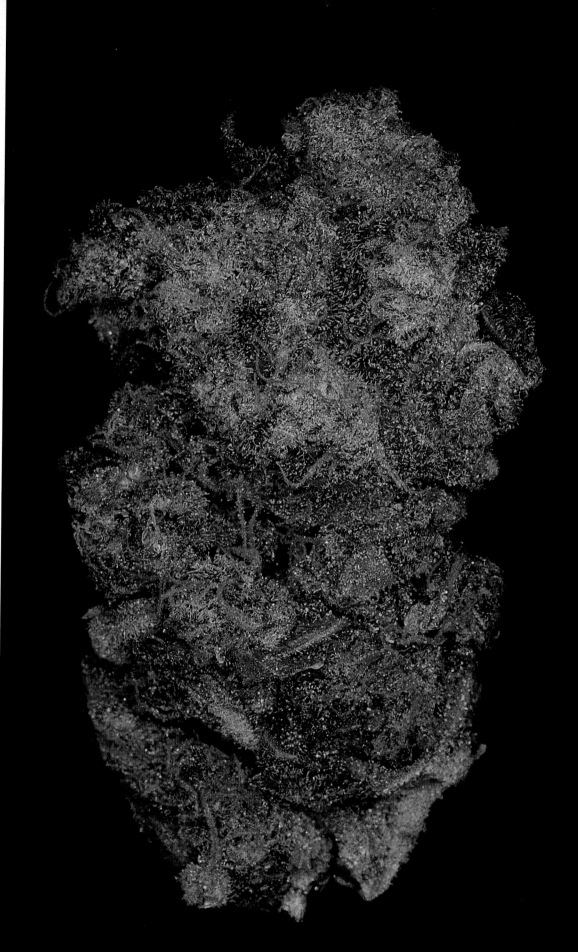

HOGSBREATH

Here is a fine example of West Coast indoor growers leading the way. This bud was grown using an organic hydroponic setup, and the quality of the smoke is exquisite—super sweet, but not the generic sweetness of so many Amsterdam strains. Every taste bud in my mouth was delighted. The high is warm and fuzzy—not overbearing. A great daytime bud. Shown on the opposite page, bottom, is a microscopic photo of Hogsbreath.

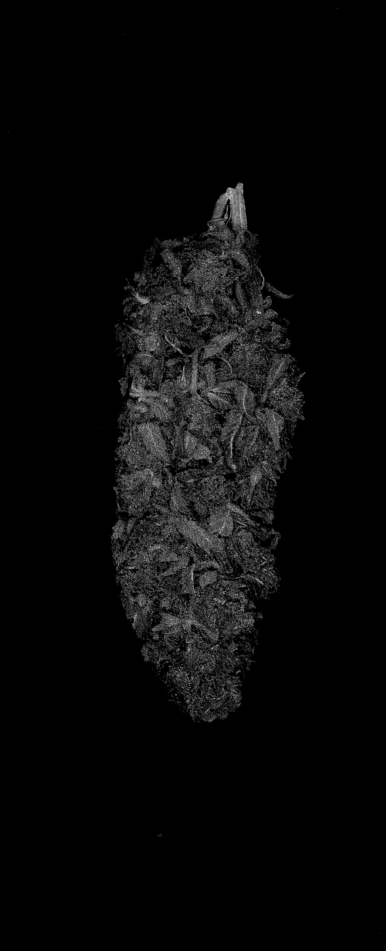

Choose Your Apparatus!

I have noticed a strange phenomenon with ganja smoking and vaporizing. It has to do with the method in which each individual strain is consumed and its perceived quality. For example, HP13 (see page 75) is truly joint bud. Sure, you could smoke it in a tin can and it would taste great, but to truly appreciate its complex flavor it must be smoked in a joint. There are tones of flavor in HP13 that simply can't be experienced any other way! Heroauna (see page 86), on the other hand, is definitely vaporizer bud. Through a joint or a bong, it just tastes like smoke. When vaporized, it releases a candied hashy flavor that makes the mouth water. Cat Piss (see page 58) can only be ultimately experienced with a large glass bong. I can't explain why, but it's true. Check it out for yourself.

humboldt

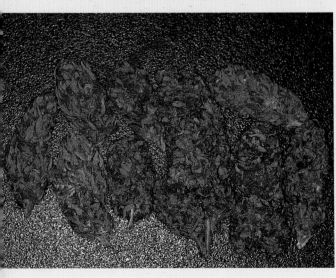

Humboldt, California, is one of the largest producers of high-grade cannabis in America, both indoors and outdoors. And while the flavors and highs of Humboldt herb are generally not overwhelming, it is regarded as some of the finest marijuana in the world. Most of the cultivators in this area have a love affair with this plant and raise it as if it were their child. Humboldt cannabis is usually very smooth with an herbal taste. The highs vary from batch to batch, but overall they are very sedating and satisfying. Most of the growers in these parts produce old sativas or indica/sativa hybrids, though many of the indoor growers are sticking to more modern strains coming through Amsterdam. (Most of which were originally West Coast strains that have been tinkered with in Holland.) Multi-pound plants are not uncommon in this marijuana-loving county, due to the ideal growing conditions and long growing season.

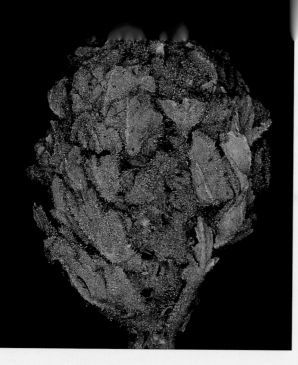

ALDER POINT

Straight out of Alder Point, this nug (above) is so earthy and robust, it begged to be rolled into a fatty and smoked. I was more than happy to oblige. The high is light, but very pleasant, with no burnout. Thanks and praises to the old schoolers who keep all these magical Californian strains going! Grown organically outdoors.

GARBERVILLE

Another original old-school Californian sativa (right), this one's lineage goes back to Mexico and Colombia. She's been in Garberville, California, since the early 1970s, though, and is definitely now considered to be Californian herb. Admittedly neither extremely potent nor flavorful, this strain brings us variety, truly the spice of life, while the indicas of today sometimes bore me.

BLACK FINGER

Yet another old Californian sativa strain, also grown outdoors organically.

HONEYDEW

This bud (left) comes from Honeydew, California. If I close my eyes and concentrate on the exhale, this bud seems to *taste* like honeydew melons. Seriously! The high is clear, focused, and light.

HUMBOLDT INDOOR

The following six samples are a good representation of the indoor Humboldt cannabis scene, which varies widely in quality. Generally speaking, most samples rate good or better, but some are downright exquisite. Overall I'm usually pretty impressed with Humboldt Indoor. Don't get me wrong; I still much prefer the outdoor, Humboldt or not. But the quality of indoor bud has steadily been getting better, and it's almost always better than the commercially produced indoor schwag being sent down from British Columbia. Diligent helicopter patrols in the last fifteen years have made many outdoor growers switch to indoor, and quality has suffered as a result, in my opinion. Many of these commercial operations are only interested in one thing—harvest size, roughly translated as dollars. Look for the smaller operations' stuff, and you are more likely to be satisfied.

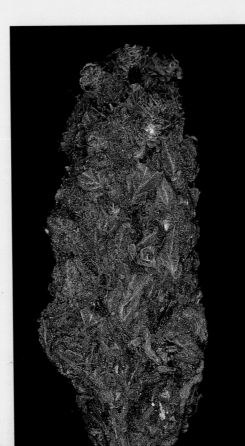

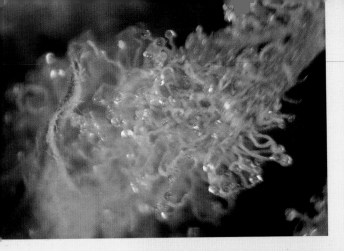

HUMBOLDT
OUTDOOR ORGANIC

These two pages present a selection of some typical, outdoor Humboldt-area herb. All samples shown were grown completely organically.

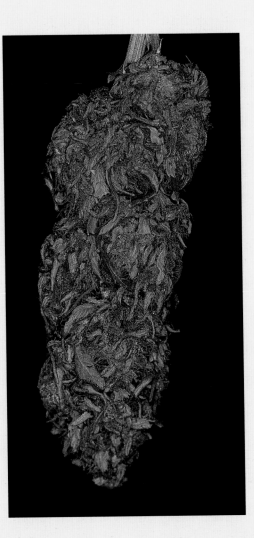

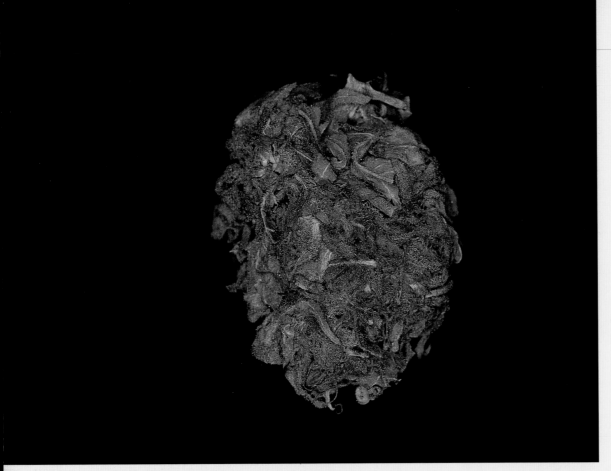

HUMBOLDT TREETOP

This is some of the finest Humboldt ganja I've ever come across. The particular batch shown on this page, at the risk of a broken neck for the grower, was grown in the tops of trees! Such extreme agriculture is evidence of just how crazy the helicopter scene is in Northern California. Nevertheless, this area is still probably the heaviest producer of domestic cannabis in America. This strain definitely has some original Haze in it (meaning pre-Amsterdam), completely evident when walking into a room where someone else is smoking it. The spicy aroma and flavor are unmistakable. Humboldt Treetop produces a soaring high, from your head to your toes. My compliments to the breeder and grower.

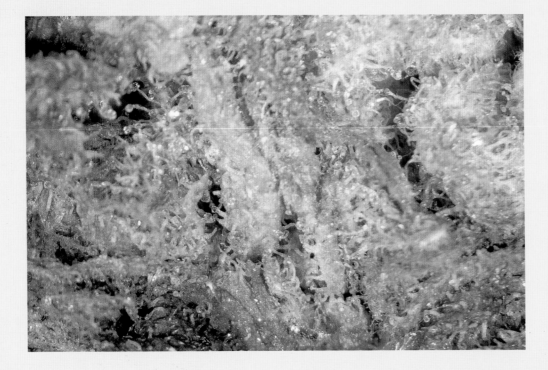

98

PURPLE HUMBOLDT

The purpleness of a bud, as shown at right, can be genetic or weather related; these were probably both.

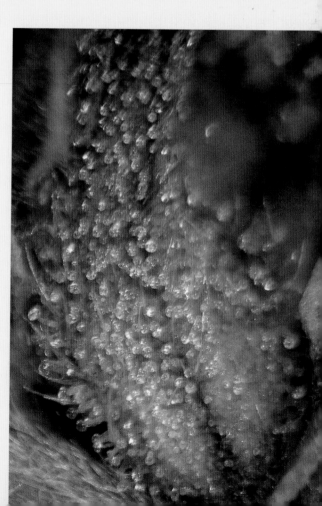

How to Properly Store Marijuana

The best way to store marijuana depends on how long you wish to store it for. Once the herb is properly dried and cured, you need to determine the expected length of storage time. For small amounts that won't last very long, a dark, dry place will be sufficient. For quantities that will last longer, such as a month, refrigeration is recommended, preferably in sealed glass jars. For amounts that will last longer than a month, freezing is the best option. Buds stored in the freezer will not deteriorate noticeably, as long as the herb isn't taken out of the freezer often. Every time it's removed from the freezer, moisture is drawn through the vegetative tissues to the outside of the buds, which can affect the taste and quality. Transferring enough stored marijuana from the freezer to the refrigerator to cover your short-term marijuana needs can cut down on the number of occasions it is taken out of the freezer. (You don't want to go into your freezer stash every time you wish to enjoy a nugget.)

ICE

This fat Paradise Seeds strain is a cross of White Widow, Special Skunk, and Northern Lights. Basically, they've taken three of the most common strains around, grown out thousands of them, and selected the best individuals for parents. I felt high just from being in the presence of this spectacular plant.

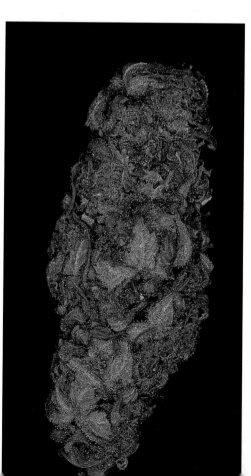

JACK FLASH

This expertly grown sample is a Sensi Seeds strain bred for Jack Herer lovers (see page 102) who desire a larger harvest. Crossed with a Super Skunk x Haze father plant, this jack-of-all-trades produces huge buds with wonderful fruity and spicy flavors. There is a lot of variety with this strain. About half the plants are very Haze/sativa influenced, taking up to eighty days to flower. The rest are indica dominated, shorter and finishing after approximately sixty days of flowering. Both phenotypes are well worth keeping. This particular sample was grown and cured to perfection, a feat rarely seen in Amsterdam. The curing is what really made this batch special. The flavor is lemony, and sort of peppery on the exhalation. The smoke is so soft and pleasant, it never bothers your throat. The high is strong and thorough, making every cell in your body feel its effects. Kudos to the growers of this fine strain, who have mastered the organic hydro method.

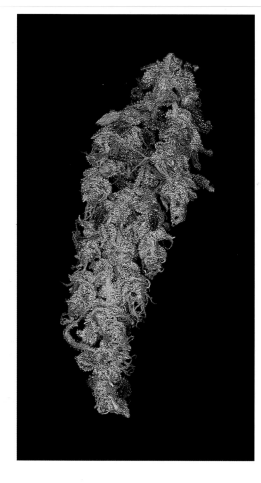

JACK HERER

Fruity and spicy—much like the man himself! Just kidding, Jack. This Sensi Seeds super-hybrid is the result of many years of selective breeding. Although I can't tell you the recipe for Coke, I can tell you that this plant is comprised of 50 percent Haze, 37.5 percent Northern Lights #5, and 12.5 percent Skunk. These three strains comprise a large percentage of the cannabis scene in Holland. All three of these strains are the result of extensive breeding projects, and the parents for Jack were selected from thousands of "brothers and sisters." In other words, if you were to cross your favorite Haze, Skunk, and Northern Lights plants, you would not end up with the same Jack. Very special plants were used to create this variety. The flavor is both fruity and spicy, and could be considered tropical. The high is very strong, with a clear sativa presence. Most coffee shops in Amsterdam have a bud called Jack Herer, but if it doesn't look like the one pictured at left, it's a fake. Winner of many Cannabis Cups, the real Jack is truly spectacular and an achievement in modern cannabis breeding.

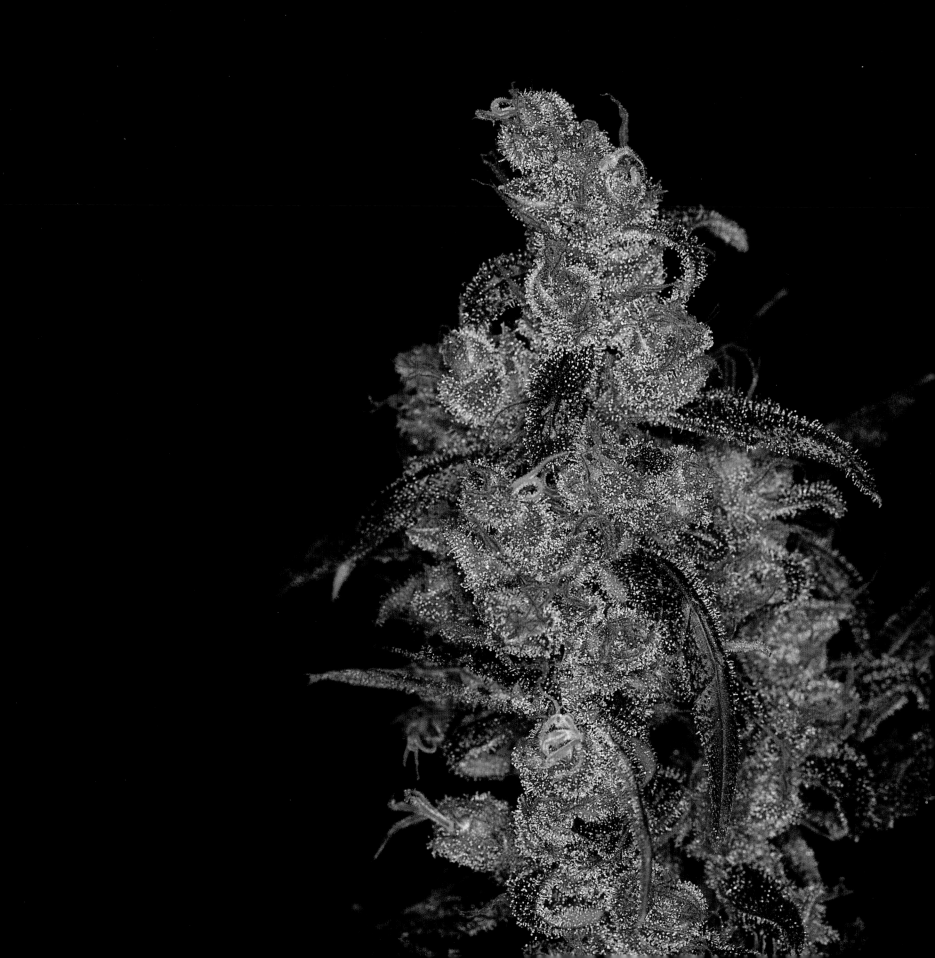

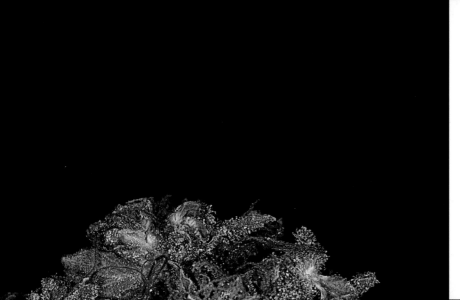

JACK HERER X HAZE

Unfortunately this extremely hazy hybrid was harvested early (notice the white hairs) and, therefore, was not up to its full potential. The aroma is spicy and intoxicating, with its Haze characteristics shining through. The high, although not fully developed, is still quite strong. The opposite page shows a microphotography shot of this strain.

JUICY FRUIT

With genetics from the Sensi Seed Bank
and grown outdoors in Hawaii, this one
(right) has real potential. Unfortunately,
she was harvested early and never reached
peak potency. Nevertheless, the flavor of
this Thai/Afghani cross is amazing; it
really tasted like Juicy Fruit gum. The high
is clear, cerebral, and very lengthy.

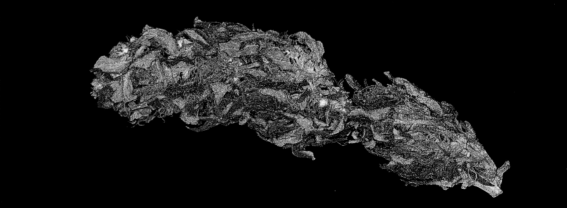

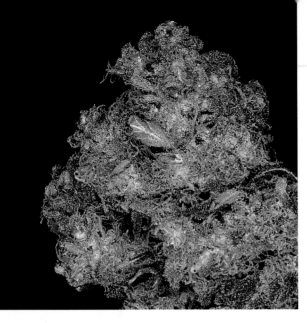

K2

This strain, photographed in Amsterdam, is reportedly a four-way cross of Northern Lights #2, Haze, Early Pearl, and Kush. Name a strain, it's in there. I found the odiferous nuggets to have a semi-cheesy smell when gently squeezed. Interesting, but I'm not sure I want my ganja to taste like cheese. The smoke is actually pretty nice; however, I found it to be a little diluted for my taste. Be aware that there is apparently more than one strain called K2.

Classy Glass

The Cannabible would not be complete without a mention of the glass paraphernalia phenomenon. It all started back in the mid-1980s when a genius glassblower named Bob Snodgrass started selling his amazing color-changing glass pipes on Grateful Dead tours. The glass doesn't actually change color, but as the resin builds up on the inside, its appearance dramatically changes, with many new features and landscapes appearing. Nearly two decades later, Snodgrass Glass is still going strong, producing some of the most mind-boggling smoking apparatuses imaginable (www.snodgrass.net). The art has progressed phenomenally, and there are now literally thousands of artists blowing glass-smoking paraphernalia with some amazing new techniques. Smoking through glass art can be an elegant experience, and it's definitely the cleanest tasting material to smoke through. With glass, you can be sure that you are only smoking your herb, and not the pipe itself. Additionally, it's easy to clean your glass with rubbing alcohol and salt. Alcohol is a solvent, and salt does not dissolve in the alcohol and acts as an abrasive, knocking off chunks of sticky resin.

ARTIST: BOB BADTRUM

ARTIST: GABRIEL

ARTIST: DANIEL CHANDLER

KALI MIST

This wonderfully exotic sativa is primarily seen in Amsterdam, unfortunately for those of us in America. What it lacks in weight it makes up for in flavor and high. These buds are lush and very exotic tasting, with a cerebral, uplifting high. Although the breeders won't give out the pedigree details, I would guess that this is a cross between Cambodian and a Haze hybrid, possibly Silver Haze. The Haze influence is unmistakable when smoked, having a glorious spiciness. These buds are stringy when growing, making it somewhat impractical for the cash cropper. Growers can choose a different strain that produces well over twice as much per plant. Kali Mist is more of a head-stash strain than a cash cropper. Kali Mist seeds are often crossed with Skunk or Afghani, making them quicker and fatter. Unfortunately, they're not even close to the pure Kali Mist experience. I recommend asking lots of questions about lineage before purchasing seeds.

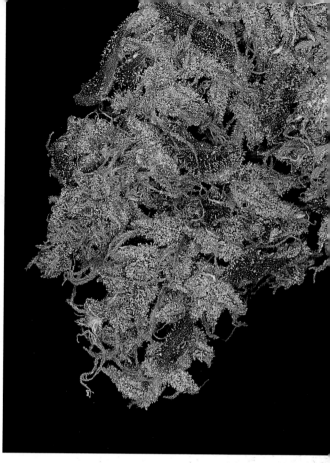

KENYAN

The plant shown on the opposite page, left, was grown from seeds taken from bricked commercial Kenyan bud scored in Europe. After traveling halfway around the world, this sativa was grown organically outdoors in Maui, Hawaii. Unique from other strains I've tried, this bud has an exquisite poison flavor, for lack of a better word, deep and thick in nature. The high is clear and very soothing, with a noticeable anti-anxiety characteristic. Although this plant was grown in nearly full sunlight, the buds are airy and light, due to genetics. Other strains grown right next to her were rock solid.

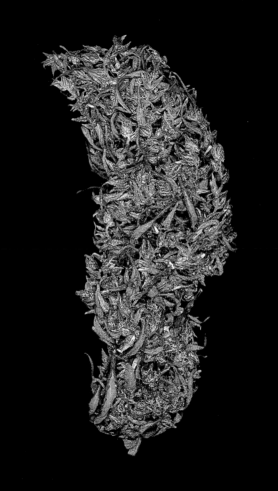

is heavy and overpowering, heralding a nice daytime nap.

MANGO BUD

This hearty outdoor bud was grown outdoors in Holland. The flavor is actually reminiscent of mangoes, or at least some type of tropical fruit. The high is lethargic and murky, pointing toward the strain's indica background.

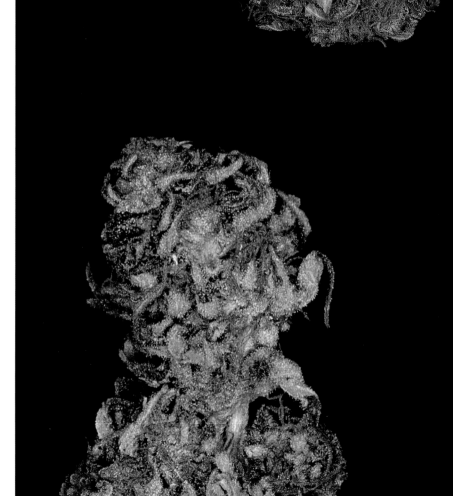

MAPLE LEAF INDICA

This monstrous indica (left) is another Sensi Seeds offering. Known to have come from Afghanistan before the Russian invasion, this strain was an important building block for many of today's most famous strains. Tangy and sweet, these buds have a lovely maple aroma and a thumping stone.

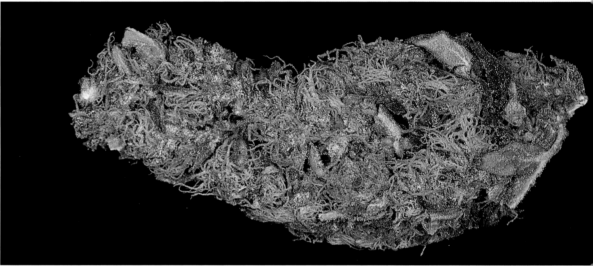

MASTER KUSH

The freakish indica shown above is the offspring of two Hindu Kush varieties, making it an F1 (first filial generation, offspring of two P1—parent—plants). Fairly high potency along with a pleasing hashy aroma and flavor make this a desirable strain. Although sometimes difficult due to its strength, the high is pleasantly heavy and giggly. Parental material comes from the Hindu Kush mountain range in Afghanistan and Pakistan. These plants would normally be used to make hash in their native countries; however, they are equally suitable for smoking as marijuana. These plants are normally short and stocky with little branching activity, making them ideal for indoor gardening. This sample was harvested prematurely, evident by the multitude of hairs that have not yet turned red, and quality suffered as a result.

This lovely array of mind-warping Hawaiian pakalolo comes from the island of Maui. Hawaiian marijuana has long been regarded as the best in the world. Is it true? Yes, most definitely, without a doubt. The flavors can be so incredibly tropical, it's like smoking a mango! Smoking some good pakalolo, which translates roughly as "crazy weed," can be a very psychedelic experience. Massive helicopter patrols combined with very little growable and accessible land that is not too crowded, along with thieves, hunters, pigs, goats, caterpillars, and much of the rest of the animal and insect kingdom make Maui the most difficult place on earth to pull off a crop. Despite this, as bad as they want it, we want it more! All samples shown were grown outdoors organically. The average harvest per plant in Maui is a measly three to fourteen grams per plant. This is due to the fact that there are four growing seasons per year, and most plants go into flowering almost immediately, while still very small. Fortunately, what they lack in size and weight, they make up in quality.

Most growers in Hawaii do not know precisely what strains they are growing. Even if they did, it wouldn't matter. Any strain grown in the islands for a few generations will begin to acclimate to the local growing conditions, which provide four or more growing seasons per year. Strains change so fast in Hawaii that after a little while, it becomes, basically, Hawaiian. That's not to say that there are no specific strains being grown there; there are many. They just might not look like they did before they were brought to Hawaii. Generally, the plants get smaller, the bracts get bigger, the flavors become tropical, and the THC content goes way up.

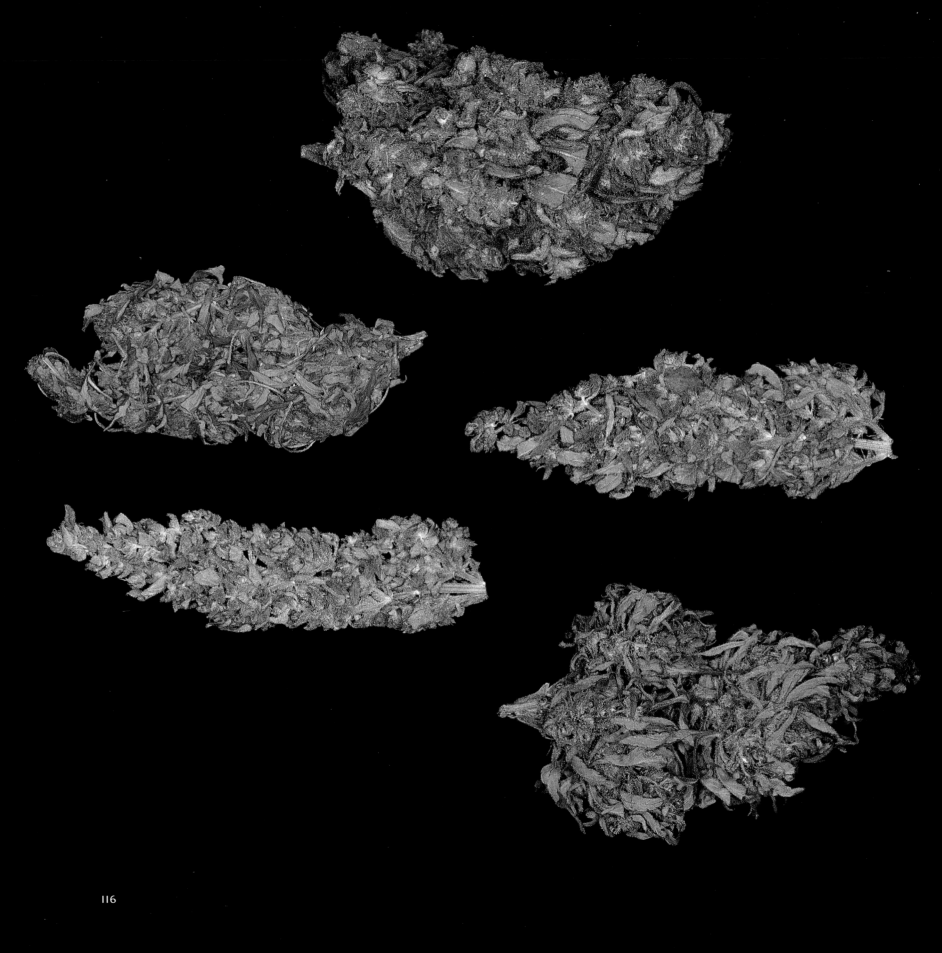

KUSH X EARLY PEARL
X HAWAIIAN LADY

121

THAI X HUMBOLDT

Clockwise from top left:

WHITE WIDOW X SKUNK

HASH PLANT X SWAZI X DUTCH

BLOOD SATIVA (AFRICAN) GROWN AT
4,500 FEET ON HALEAKALA VOLCANO

Vaporization

Vaporization, a technique that was pioneered in the '60s, is a process that heats herb to the point where the active constituents are released but nothing is burned (approximately 360°F). When used properly, a vaporizer releases no carcinogens, tar, or other irritants, thereby eliminating most of the negative effects of smoking, which is the whole point: There is no smoke!

Until recently, most vaporizers had a heating element, a tray, and a collection chamber. These devices were clumsy, somewhat wasteful, not very effective, and, consequently, not much fun. Vaporizing technology has been steadily improving, and thanks to some clever researchers, it is ready for mainstream use. I use an SVT, or Superior Vaporization Technique, promoted by VripTech International. The SVT employs an industrial heat gun with ceramic-encapsulated heating elements to ensure a long tool life and clean, nonmetallic heat; a glass bong; and a specially made two-piece glass bowl (available at www.vriptech.com).

The heat gun blows hot air over the herb and vaporizes the resin glands right off their stalks. Since vaporization takes place at temperatures below pyrolysis (combustion) twice as many active constituents are delivered to the user than one would get from smoking, according to studies. (Cannabinoids are highly combustible, and many of the delicate resin-producing glandular trichomes are destroyed when smoked.)

Many people are surprised to learn that I use no water in my bong when vaporizing. According to a marijuana water-pipe and vaporizer study done by the Multidisciplinary Association for Psychedelic Studies (MAPS) and the National Organization for the Reform of Marijuana Laws (NORML), water tends to absorb THC more readily than it absorbs noxious tars. At first, I didn't believe it either, but I must say, removing the water from my bong when vaporizing does produce stronger effects and even more flavor. When taking a vrip—vaporized rip—the SVT folks recommend using scissors to first break up the bud and expose more surface area to the heat. I prefer to place a small piece of bud in the bowl—some precious resin could stick to the scissors or fall off the bud. After my first vrip, I flip the bud over and take another vrip from the other side. Next, I crush the dry and crumbly herb in the bowl into near powder, thus exposing most of the vegetative matter for easy vaporization. One final vrip leaves me with a pile of resinless vegetative matter. Careful microscope examination of this final material, called LC or load carcass, shows that approximately 90 to 95 percent of the resin has been vaporized.

This bud had two vrips taken off of it, effectively vaporizing approximately 85 percent of the resin.

Since vaporization delivers twice as many actives as smoking, it represents a significant financial savings, especially given the price of marijuana these days! Though vaporizing should reduce the amount of herb consumed by half, I still seem to go through more herb when vaporizing. The reason is as follows: If I smoke marijuana, I often cough so much that my throat and lungs cannot handle any more. When I vaporize, however, it's so easy on the body that I can just keep on going—and because the taste is so sublime, I usually do!

Vaporization also reduces the headache factor. If I smoke all day long, I often end up with an achy head and a stiff body. Vaporizing greatly reduces this problem. Vaporizing also seems to change the character of the high experienced. It is a cleaner and more functional high than one from smoking. It makes an indica feel like a sativa, a welcome change in my book.

MEAN GREEN

This beautiful redhead has an incredibly sweet, almost bubblegum taste and smell. Claimed to be over twenty years old, it makes a great daytime bud with a light, yet focused high. This batch was grown in a hydroponic system, and the fertilizers were well flushed, making for a smooth and delightful smoke.

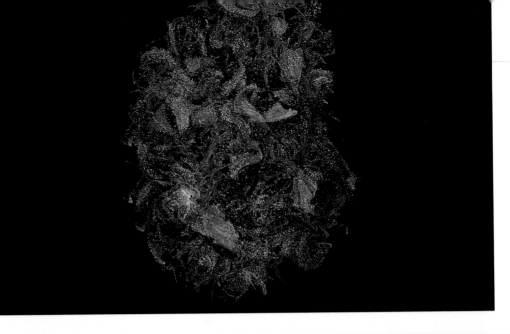

mendocino

Mendocino County, located several hours north of the San Francisco Bay Area, produces some of the most beautiful nugs in the world. Mendocino (outdoor) buds are usually very dense and large, and it is not uncommon for plants grown in this area to harvest two to four pounds each due mostly to the area's fantastic growing conditions. Mendocino probably has the most progressive marijuana laws in the country, having recently decriminalized possession of up to twenty-five plants. These relaxed laws have inspired many a Mendo grower to plant in full sunlight, right in backyards in many cases. This area is so fueled by marijuana commerce, that you can literally feel it in the air.

INDOOR MENDOCINO I

Although this cannabis looks quite nice, with its vivid colors and pretty red hairs, it is completely unimpressive when smoked. It has a boring, lightly sweet taste and an almost undetectable high. Grown indoors commercially in Mendocino, California, this bud is typical of commercially produced, warehouse-grown indoor marijuana. It is shown as an example of what I call "chemmy indoor no-love schwag." These buds get a "looks can be deceiving" award.

MENDOCINO GREENHOUSE WITH SUPPLEMENTAL LIGHTS

This is another boring commercial Mendocino strain. These plants are grown in a greenhouse with supplemental lighting. While these buds look and smell quite nice, the flavor and high are most unimpressive. These buds also get a "looks can be deceiving" award.

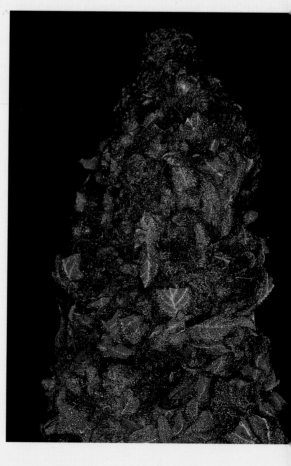

MENDOCINO OUTDOOR ORGANIC

This selection of outdoor grown Mendo-cino nuggets is a fair representation of Mendo's finest. All samples shown are completely organic, duly noted at every inhalation of the mind-numbing smoke. Most of these strains are old-school sativas and have been grown in this area for decades. The plants shown on the opposite page were grown from seeds taken from the buds shown on the opposite page, lower left, and grown outdoors organically in Maui.

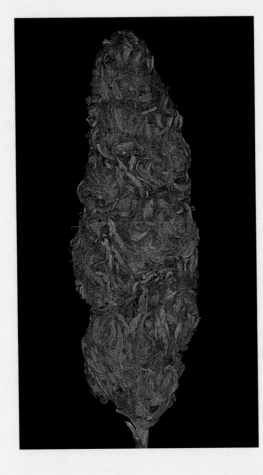

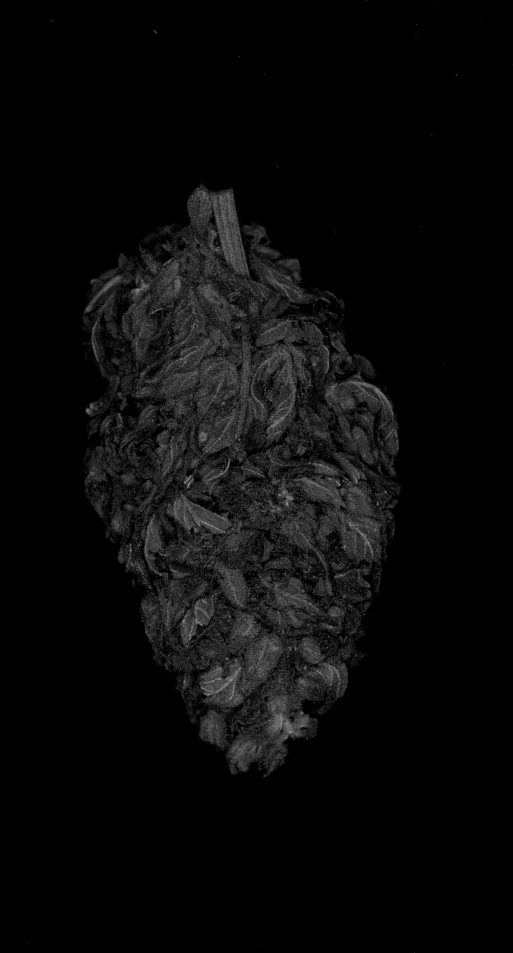

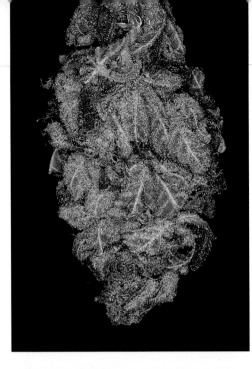

MERRY CRYSTAL

This gorgeous specimen is a member of the White Russian family. Expressing both sides of the indica/sativa spectrum, Merry Crystal, a Greenhouse Seed Company strain, seems to drip resin. The aromatic flowers are soft and sweet, typical of the White line, though they have a tangy and noticeably different aftertaste. The stone is strong, though it could be stronger.

MISTY

Misty is an Amsterdam strain that is closely related to White
Widow; she's her sister, so to speak. Misty, however, is more stable
than her Widow sister. This one's so sweet smelling it almost seems
putrid, but I actually like it. Grown indoors in Holland, this bud
has a heavy and cloudy munchy-inducing high that ends with a
huge pig out.

Cannabis Etiquette

Marijuana smoking is very much a social thing, and it's important to be respectful and courteous to others when partaking in this sacred ceremony. This can be challenging while traveling, because cannabis etiquette varies from region to region. For example, in California, a bong hit is a one-person thing. If you take a hit from the bong and then try to pass it to someone, they will most likely stare at you blankly, wondering why you are trying to get them to "take out your trash." If you consider that the first hit is the most potent and by far the tastiest, this practice makes sense. On the East Coast, however, if you pass someone a half-smoked bong hit, most likely they will be stoked just to smoke some pot! In America, most people share joints in a group. In Amsterdam, Jamaica, and much of the rest of the world, one joint is for one person. If you asked someone for a hit off of theirs, they would probably wonder why you didn't just roll your own. In many of Asia's hashiest countries, most cannabis lovers don't even smoke marijuana, considering it to be a crude and unfinished product. They only smoke hash. Since every region has its own code, just be polite and ask before making any assumptions, and you should be *irie* in no time!

MOLASSES

This Southern California strain has a thick, syrupy flavor that justifies its name. Despite the sample being a little too dry, an abundance of gooey flavor was present. A look under the microscope (below) reveals a dense forest of glistening, fat resin glands.

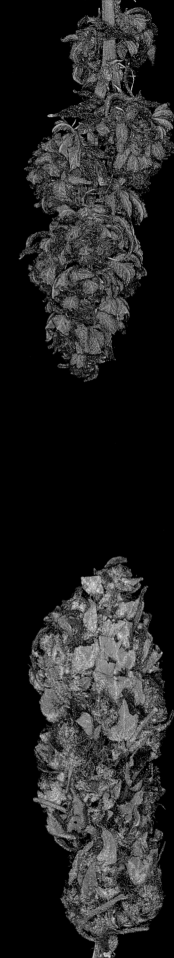

MOLOKAI YELLOW

Located just across the channel from Maui, Molokai is a lovely little island paradise. The bud shown is an old Molokai strain, grown conscientiously and lovingly. This nectarous strain produces a heavy stone that is very meditative and peaceful. The flavor is lemony, spicy, and creamy, much like a Citral strain, and with definite bubblegum overtones.

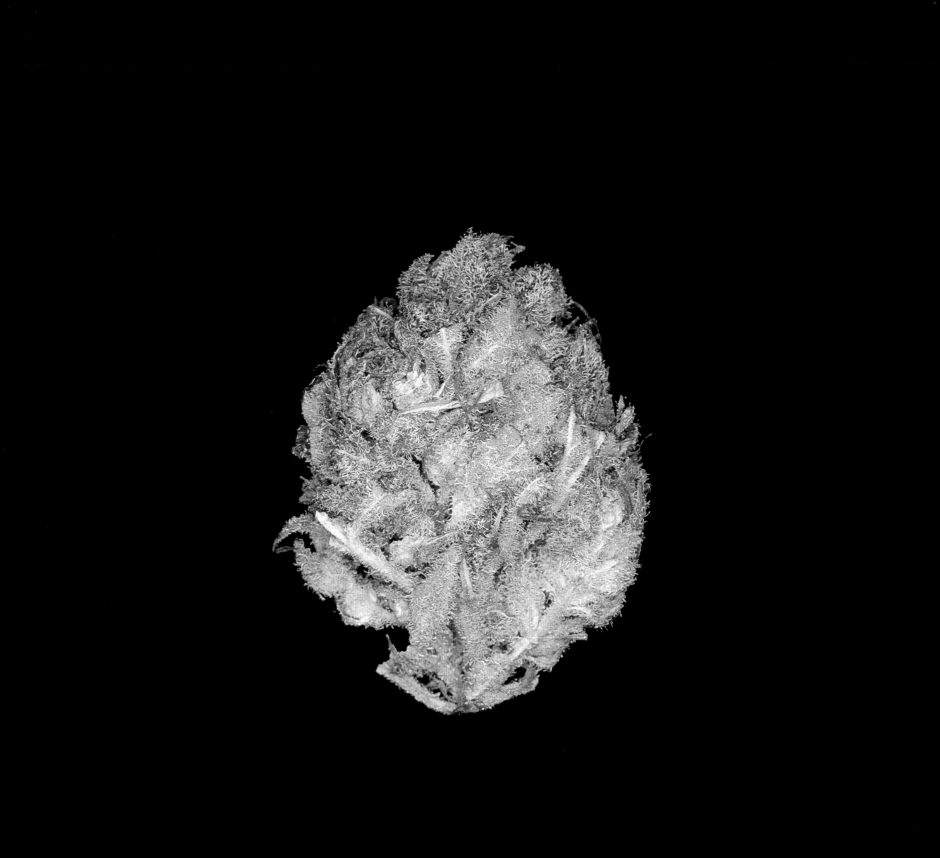

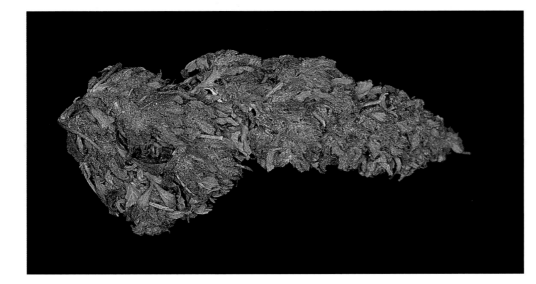

MT. SHASTA

This bud was grown outdoors organically in the Mt. Shasta area of Northern California. Thick, rich, skunky smoke leads to a powerful head buzz that lasts all afternoon. Northern California still produces the fattest buds around.

MYSTIQUE

This pure sativa (opposite page) was grown indoors in Amsterdam. Genetic details remain a mystery for now. This one is totally different from anything I've come across. The smoke is distinctive in flavor: dry, peppery, and musky all in one. The high is very cerebral, a clear sign of sativa lineage. Giant golden resin glands attached to long white stalks weave a magnificent jungle of psychedelic wonder before your very eyes. Absolutely beautiful.

NIGERIAN SILK

Grown hydroponically in New York City, this sativa strain is supposedly from Nigeria. I couldn't confirm this, but the flavor is different than anything else I've tasted. Do you believe?

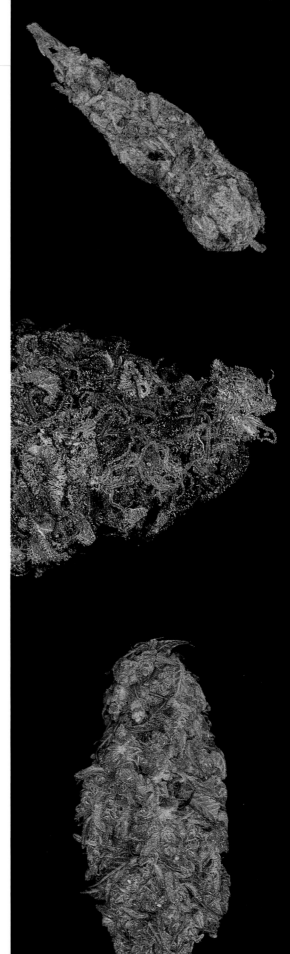

NORTHERN LIGHTS

Quite possibly the most famous marijuana strain in existence, Northern Lights, a clone bred in the Pacific Northwest, is a highly inbred Afghani. This classic indica strain was tweaked for over twenty generations before being released to the public, although it never became stable like Skunk No. 1. The plants grow short and compact, with a giant cola on top. While Northern Lights is highly adapted to indoor growing, fantastic outdoor batches also can be grown. Although this strain is incredibly resinous, I usually find the flavor of Northern Lights to be a little lacking. The high, on the other hand, is not lacking at all. It is a typical indica high, narcotic and dreamy.

A Northern Lights stem, coated in glistening resin glands.

NORTHERN LIGHTS X BLUEBERRY

This stunning hybrid is the result of crossing a pure Northern Lights plant with a pure Blueberry one. The resin is really oozing in this fine specimen. Grown hydroponically indoors, this is truly a connoisseur's delight. This bud leaves a sweet blueberry taste in the mouth while producing a knockout indica buzz. Judging by the complex yet smooth character of the smoke, I would guess that it was grown organically.

NORTHERN LIGHTS X HAZE (CALIFORNIA)

This bud (far right) is reported to have been grown outdoors in California, but something about the funky flavor leaves me doubting this story. Some of the buds were completely infested with bugs— mostly aphids, but some spider mites were also present. The taste is chalky, for lack of a better word, and somewhat unpleasant. The high is dreary and clumsy. Not recommended for vegetarians. It is important to note that NL x HZ is a fantastic strain. The growing situation held this one back.

NORTHERN LIGHTS X HAZE (AMSTERDAM)

Originally introduced by the Seed Bank in 1988, this is a hybridized cross of two of the most famous strains in existence, Northern Lights and Haze. The NL was used to bring the Haze's extremely long flowering time down to acceptable levels, making it suitable for indoor growing. The buds are sweet, pungent, fruity, and spicy, with a heavy spicy aftertaste. The Haze's soaring cerebral high really shines through here; however, the NL's indica influence adds some body to the mix. This light-loving strain is not recommended for lightweights!

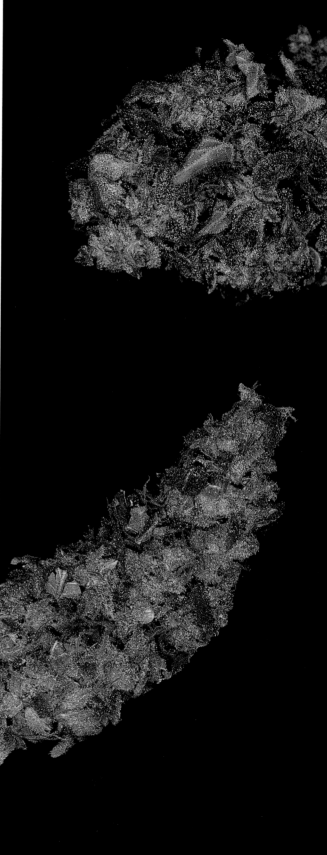

Worms left a trail of rot and death in their wake.

The enemy in action.

Stress of the attack caused this plant to turn purple and finish early.

Microphotography of a live plant

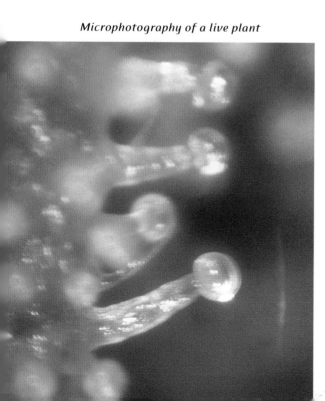

NORTHERN LIGHTS X HAZE X HASH PLANT

This is world-class marijuana. The parents used to create this hybrid were very special indeed. They were selected from tens of thousands of "brothers and sisters." Crops are shown from two different years both grown in Southern California. The second year's crop was badly damaged due to a worm infestation (upper right). The problem started out as small white balls on the plant. Within days, the plants freaked out and turned purple, and the little balls became little worms. Soon after that, the worms became caterpillars, and they left an inch-thick trail of rot and death in their wake. The plants, in shock, finished nearly two weeks early and were basically dying on the stem. Despite the worm problem, both year's crops were phenomenal, but the first year's crop was better. They taste very purple, very creamy, and very spicy. This fine ganja was cured for over two months, which is apparent in the mind-numbing smoke. This hybrid became extinct following a raid on medical-marijuana activist Todd McCormick, who is still in prison.

NORTHERN LIGHTS #5

Northern Lights #5 is a truly awesome strain. Twenty years of selective inbreeding produced this highly celebrated plant. Originally available from the Sensi Seed Bank, NL5 is a crossing of a pure Northern Lights male with a Northern Lights (75 percent)/Thai (25 percent) female. The compact indica strain was bred for vigorous growth, high yield, and strength of high. This variety is incredibly resinous, with a pungent sweetness that must be experienced to be believed. The Thai influence, as small as it is, has a wondrous effect on the Northern Lights mom. Two versions of NL5 are pictured: Both were outstanding, but the version shown at lower left on page 141 flowered for three additional weeks and received a proper three-month cure. The difference is profound. Subtle tones of flavor are easily noticeable with the longer cure. The smoke is incredibly rich, especially for Amsterdam bud. Top honors indeed. Scored at the Katsu coffee shop in Amsterdam, which specializes in Hazes, these buds are extraordinary and exotic.

NORTHERN LIGHTS #5 X HAZE (INDOOR)

This outstanding hybrid has long been one of my personal favorites. When grown properly, NL5 x Haze is so strong that its potency often surprises experienced smokers. The Haze brings a wicked spiciness to the palate, while the NL5 reduces the flowering time and the plant's size while keeping the potency extremely high. Overall, the high leans toward the sativa end of the spectrum, heady and cerebral in nature. The narcotic-like indica aspect is definitely there as well, although not as pronounced as the sativa, depending of course on seed or clone selection. This strain is a perfect example of hybrid vigor, a condition that exists when two different gene pools are crossed. Simply put, the best aspects of both parents are often expressed. Versions of outdoor Maui (below) and indoor Maui (left) are shown, with the outdoor Maui being the obvious winner by a factor of ten. These plants were clones taken from the same mother.

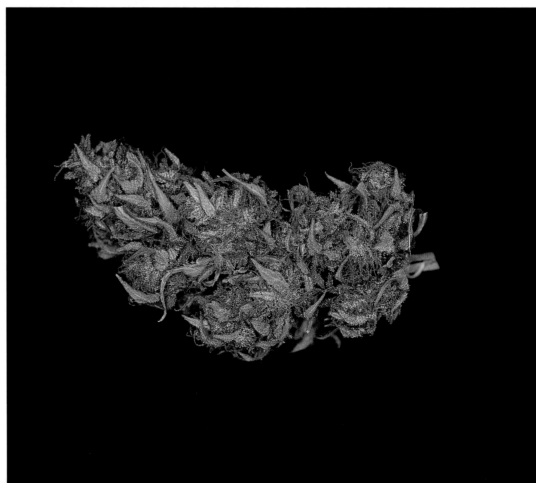

NORTHERN LIGHTS #6

This sparkling indica was grown hydroponically in the San Francisco Bay Area as medicine
for a cannabis buyers club. Trichome Technologies, the breeders, had it tested at over 22
percent THC. Please keep in mind that this NL6 is from Trichome Tech, not from Sensi
Seeds. I found this Northern Lights selection to be of higher quality than any Northern
Lights I've tried in Amsterdam. The high is extremely strong, yet manageable.

ORANGE BUD

Here is a very red, very boring Skunk variety from Amsterdam (below, left). Yes, the red hairs are pretty, but they're not psychoactive. Completely generic in all respects, the only thing I liked about this bud was the lichen-like growth of the dried red pistils, which I had never seen before.

OREGON GOLD

This beautiful West Coast strain is a hybrid containing Hawaiian, G13, and an old Asian strain. The buds have a distinctive flavor, with many subtle and exotic overtones. Sweet, sour, spicy—it all seemed to be in there. The high was clean and soaring, reminiscent of the fine sativas of the '70s. Bravo.

PALM SPRINGS OUTDOOR

Here's a crop produced by a major outdoor
growing operation near Palm Springs, California. The buds look and smell pretty
nice, but a closer inspection reveals that
many of the gland heads are missing. I sus-
pect either that the handling was
extremely rough, believable because of the
remote growing location, or someone's
making lots of (low-quality) "kif," more
properly named, resin powder. This is a
lame practice because it effectively cuts the
marijuana. Overall, these commercially
produced buds were uninteresting and of
average potency.

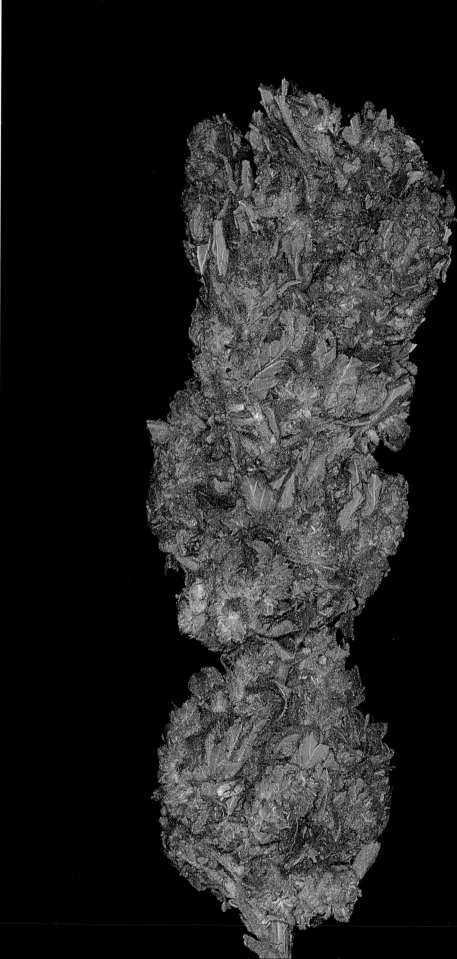

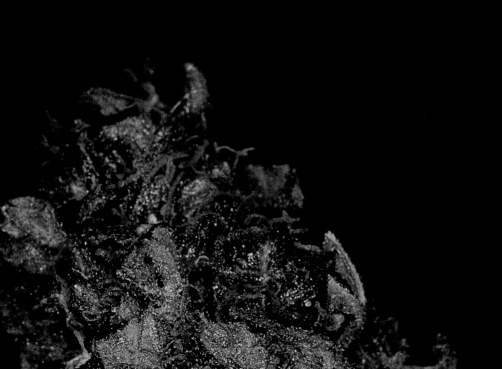

PURPLE HAZE

"Purple Haze . . . was in my brain." A strain worthy of Jimi? Maybe. This one is most likely a cross of Purple Power and Purple Star, both of which can be recognized in the bud's structure and flavor. Unfortunately, this is probably not the famous Purple Haze of the '70s. I'm afraid that one's long gone. This one is spicy and very purple tasting, though a bit rough. The high is fairly weak in comparison to all the other nugs floating around Amsterdam.

PURPLE KUSH

This rotund nugget (opposite page, upper left) is a proud offering from Trichome Technologies. These guys are scientific about their work, and it shows in the quality of the buds. Thick, musky, spicy smoke kissed my lungs as my eyes started turning red. The high that immediately followed was heavy and mellow, almost opiate-like. Two factors can produce purple buds: cold weather or genetics. In this case, it was genetics. Tested at 16.1 percent THC, this Kush was grown hydroponically in the San Francisco Bay Area.

PURPLE PINOCCHIO

Photographed at the Greenhouse Seed Company breeding facility, this purple-tinged beauty (opposite page, right) has a uniquely seductive flavor not unlike grapes. The high is cerebral, indicating a mostly sativa gene pool. She was grown indoors in Amsterdam.

PURPLE POWER

This old-school strain (opposite page, lower left) is hearty enough to be grown outdoors in cold climates like Amsterdam. Due to its relatively easy outdoor growing, Purple Power is cheap and abundant in Holland. Many people grow a few plants on their roof. The flavor is sweet and cinnamon, with a purple presence. The high is mellow, clear, and perfect for daytime if you're a lightweight.

PURPLE STAR

Ah, the king of the Purples. This hardy outdoor strain was bred and grown in Holland. This herb is almost always available and very inexpensive in Holland since almost anyone can grow it outdoors with minimal investment. (Most cannabis in Holland is grown indoors, requiring much more of an outlay than dirt and some buckets.) This indica is so purple that it often appears black! It doesn't have the smoothest taste, probably because amateurs normally grow it. The flavor is strong and quite spicy, but a little rough. The high is decent, but nothing to write home about.

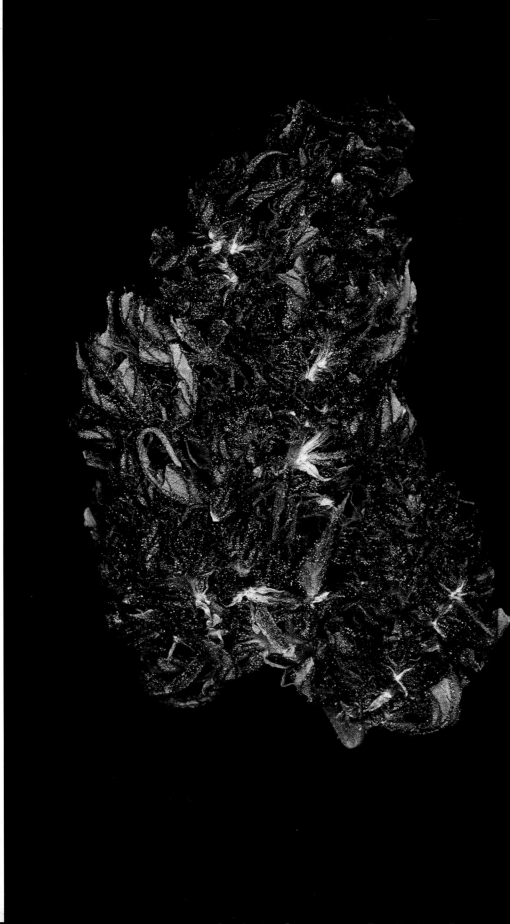

QUEEN

This hybrid strain is a cross between an Afghani and a Big Bud plant. Hybrid vigor has been achieved with these fat ladies. The plants finish relatively quickly, and the yield is high. Grown indoors hydroponically in perlite, vermiculite, and cactus sand, these buds have a sweet and slightly pungent flavor. It is likely that the weaker and redder Dutch Big Bud was used here. This cross is local to the Southern California area.

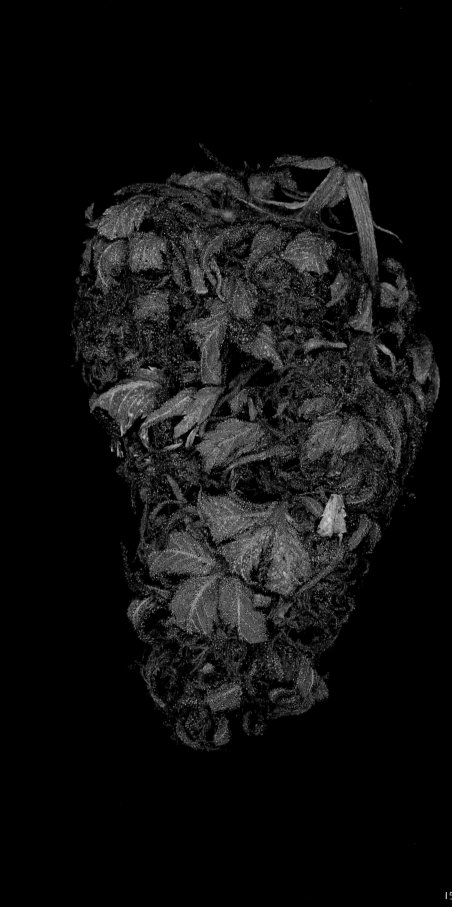

THE REAL McCOY

When I first tried The Real McCoy (left and opposite page, left), a Flying Dutchmen Seed Company offering, it seemed familiar. It reminded me of an old Hawaiian strain I see every once in a while. When I investigated the strain's lineage, I learned that it was in fact descendant from an old Hawaiian strain. The flavor of this variety is unique; it has a balmy sort of muskiness, sometimes with mango overtones. The high is quite strong and is felt mostly in the head.

RUDERALIS X INDICA

Ruderalis is a weedy variety of cannabis coming mostly from Russia and other parts of central and eastern Europe. The strain lacks potency but is very useful to breeders trying to create strains suitable for growing in extreme northern climates. Usually finishing in July, Ruderalis appears to be the earliest-harvesting outdoor strain on the planet; however, the plants generally do not ripen evenly. In this hybrid (lower left), Ruderalis was crossed with a potent indica, creating a hybrid with decent potency and flavor, and a late-August harvest time. Very respectable indeed, but unless the climate you live in demands such a strain, a much tastier variety would be preferable.

RUSSIAN OUTDOOR

These buds (opposite page, right) were reported to have been grown in Perestrojka, Russia. I got them from a Russian, so that makes it a little more believable. Do you believe? Though the flavor and high were mild, the exotic factor definitely made smoking the herb enjoyable.

SAGE

This stunning strain (right) is from the T. H. Seeds collection in Amsterdam. Sage is a Haze hybrid with roots reaching back to old-school California days; I believe there is some Big Sur Holy Weed in there. T. H. Seeds is one of very few companies bringing new genetics to Holland, a much-needed feat. Recommended. One side note: Sage-2-0, hash made from Sage with an Ice-o-Lator hash-making device, was the tastiest treat going around at the 1999 Cannabis Cup. Top honors!

SENSI STAR

This compact and fruity indica plant (left) is another fine offering from Paradise Seeds. Winner of the High Life Cup in '99, Sensi Star is proving to be one of the finest strains in Amsterdam. The High Life Cup is much more impartial than the High Times Cannabis Cup; tests are done double blind-folded, so the judges don't know what strain they are judging. In other words, it is not just an ass-kissing festival. These buds are heavily laden with resin, and produce a deeply narcotic-feeling buzz.

SHIVA SHANTI

This three-way hybrid (lower left, opposite page) consists mostly of an old Afghani strain called Garlic Bud. An old favorite from the Sensi Seed Bank, Shiva Shanti has a thick, penetrating aroma, with not-so-subtle hints of skunkiness. The high is heady and of medium strength. Shiva Shanti is a nice solid indica. Shivanti, a similar strain, is also pictured (opposite page, upper left).

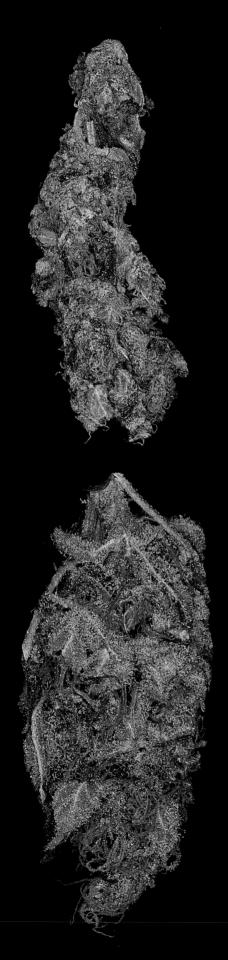

SHIVA SKUNK

Shiva Skunk is a cross of two of the most famous strains in existence—Skunk No. 1 and Northern Lights #5. Two versions are pictured: a California organic hydro batch (opposite page, upper left), and an Amsterdam bio batch, which was most likely not organic (opposite page, lower left and right). Although the California Shiva was harvested early, it was still the superior bud. Because it was organic, I could easily detect the complexity of flavors in the sweet, almost milky-tasting smoke. The exhale, strangely, was more on the skunky side. Unfortunately, probably due to the premature harvesting, finishing the bowl didn't taste so nice. This herb's high is light, clean, and uplifting. Some people like the lighter high of a premature plant, but I don't. Because of the early harvest, the high was not completely developed, and the resin glands were accordingly small. The Amsterdam Shiva was also nice, but due to the chemical fertilizers used, it lacked the mouthwatering flavor of the Californian. The two, in fact, barely seem related. It is possible, however, that the California grower simply made a better selection (from Amsterdam seed!) than the Amsterdam grower did. Remember—every seed is a different potential brother or sister.

SILVER HAZE

Another fine Sensi Seeds strain, Silver Haze is a cross of Silver Pearl and Haze. Although not a huge producer, the buds are of incredible quality and reek with Haze spiciness. The indica's early-flowering characteristic does not diminish the Haze's soaring sativa high. Three different versions are shown: Amsterdam Hydro (opposite page, bottom), Amsterdam Bio (right, bottom), and California outdoor organic (opposite page, top). While both of the Amsterdam versions are outstanding, the California outdoor is easily my favorite. For one thing, it stayed lit and burned properly. Besides that, the organic smoke felt much more comfortable in my throat and lungs. The benefits of organic growing are endless, but the true test comes at the end of the day. After a day of smoking the outdoor, my head was clean and clear, with no signs of burnout or headache. Truly a connoisseur's delight.

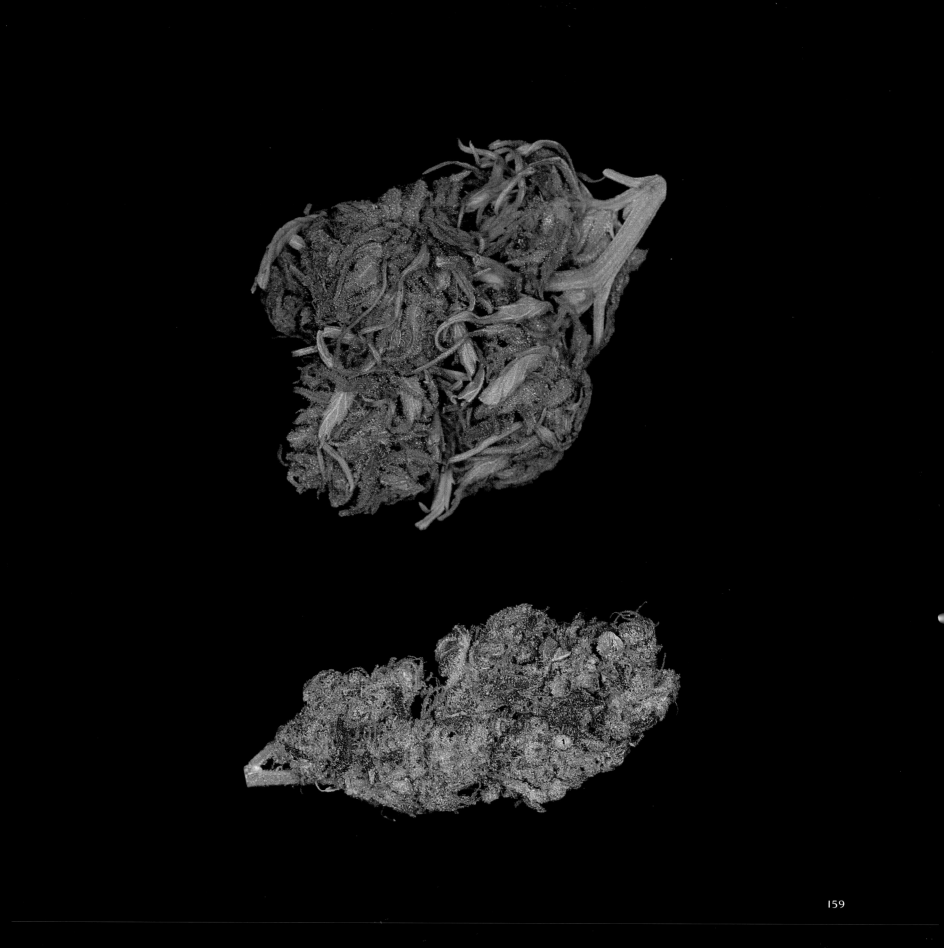

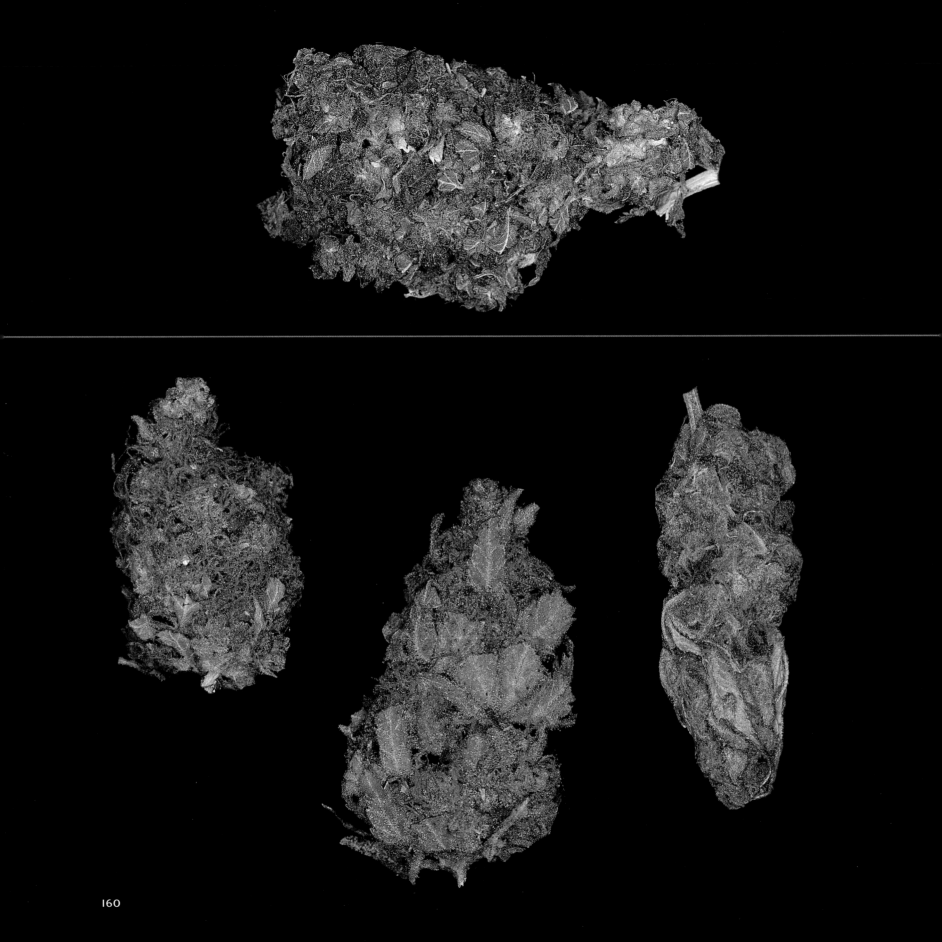

SILVER PEARL

Silver Pearl is a Sensi Seeds offering that combines some of the best strains around. An Early Pearl/Skunk No. 1 male was used with a pure Northern Lights #5 female. To delve further into the strain's lineage, Early Pearl is a crossing of Pollyanna, a sativa from the '70s, and Early Girl, a cross of Afghani and Mexican. Skunk No. 1 is a four-way hybrid containing Afghani, Acapulco Gold, Colombian, and Thai. Northern Lights #5 is a highly inbred Northern Lights with a slight Thai influence. So as you can see, many gene pools have contributed to Silver Pearl. The flavor of this exquisite strain is something like incense and toffee. The high is strong, but rather generic in nature.

SKUNK NO. I

Skunk No. 1 is the backbone of the modern cannabis breeding world. Created about twenty years ago in California, and heavily inbred since, Skunk No. 1 is now a stable and true-breeding strain. Originally a three-way, now it's most often seen as a four-way cross between Afghani, Acapulco Gold, Colombian, and Thai, making it 75 percent sativa. For some strange reason, there is a huge difference between the Skunk in Holland and in America. In Holland, the Skunk is an extremely sweet smelling and tasting plant. In America, however, the Skunk is acrid and, well, skunky! The only logical explanation for this is that the breeders in Holland selected for sweetness while the breeders in America selected for skunkiness. I much prefer the American version. Shown are the boring red Amsterdam Skunk (opposite page, bottom left), a Sensi Seeds Skunk grown indoors hydroponically in Humboldt (opposite page, bottom center), and a Skunk grown indoors in British Columbia (oppostie page, bottom right)—the best of the three but still not even close to California Skunk.

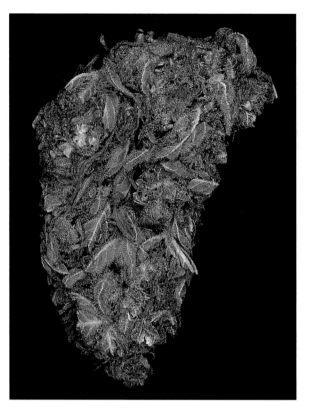

SKUNK PASSION

Another of the endless Skunk varieties, Skunk Passion was bred for early-flowering characteristics. This mostly sativa strain produces nice, fat buds with a sweet and slightly skunky flavor, though it's not as intense as an American Skunk. The high is mellow and quite average, and left me craving some serious nugs.

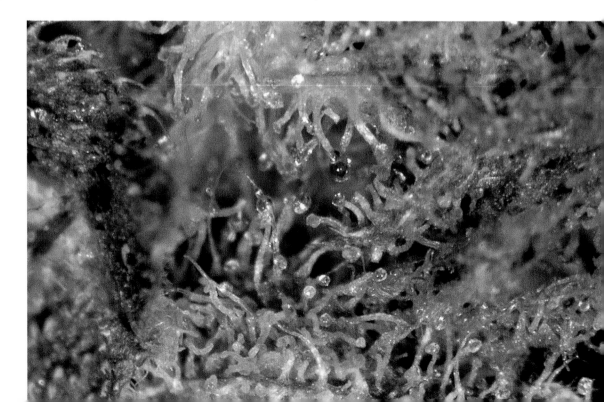

Grown outdoors organically in Maui

SOUR DIESEL

Straight out of New York City, this strain is completely unlike anything else I've tried. The flavor is absolutely brilliant, bringing back childhood memories of all the candy I ever ate. Sour D, as the people lucky enough to have the strain sometimes call it, tastes like Lemonheads candy. It's the sandalwood, tangy lemon thing that makes you want to never stop exhaling. This stuff is worth smoking for flavor alone, although the thick, powerful indica high is also very impressive. Chem and a Massachusetts Super Skunk, completely different (and better) than the Amsterdam Super Skunk, were the parents used to create Sour D. This is one more reminder that the best indoor herb is, in fact, not coming out of Amsterdam.

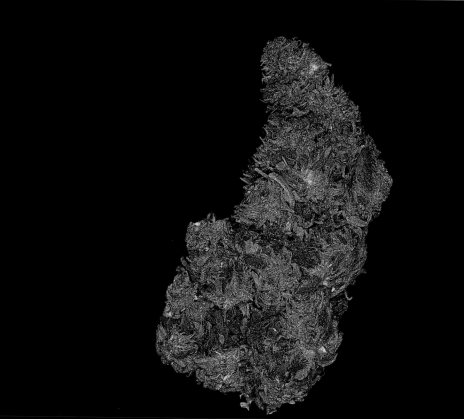

SOUTHERN CALIFORNIA DESERT

This strain was specially bred to survive the harsh conditions of the deserts in Southern California. There's some Hawaiian in there, a little Northern Lights, and perhaps another couple of unknown strains. In consideration of the large amounts these folks grow, the quality is quite good. The flavor leans toward the skunky acrid side, with hashy overtones. The high is average, with a little indica murkiness.

STRETCH

This fluffy indoor-grown nugget was picked up in the San Diego area. Genetic information is not available. A tangy and slightly minty smoke is followed nicely by a heady and intellectually charged buzz. Bravo.

SUPER HAZE

Here is another stunning Haze selection from the Katsu coffee shop in Amsterdam. These guys really know Hazes. This hybrid is a crossing of Super Skunk and Haze. The Haze spiciness is very pronounced in this fine ganja. A clear and energetic high stayed with me most of the afternoon after a spliff. These suckers have an overwhelming reek; they are herbal and spicy and everything nicey.

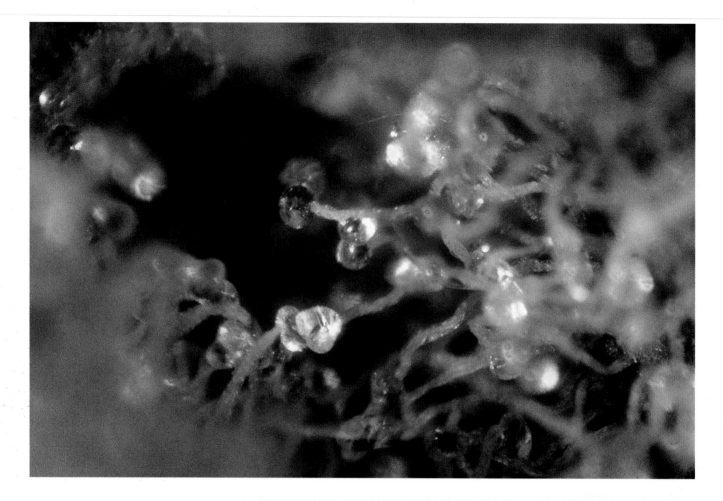

SUPER SHIVA

This golf-ball-sized nugget has a beautiful, supersweet, somewhat tangy flavor. The high is about average in intensity, though a little cloudy for my personal preferences. The strain is a hybridized cross of Super Skunk and Shiva Skunk, though it did not taste skunky at all. Grown hydroponically indoors in Holland, this is typical of Amsterdam Skunks.

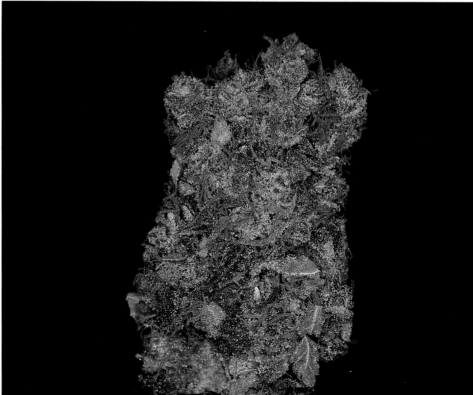

SUPER SILVER HAZE

Winner of the ultimate Cannabis Cup in '98 and '99, Super Silver Haze is about the closest most people will get to smoking pure Haze nowadays. These buds have an incredibly spicy aroma, and the flavor will leave a smile on your face for hours. The high from this cannabis is extraordinarily strong. It can break through any weak lingering high from another strain. The genetics used in this plant came from the three most celebrated cannabis strains of all time—Skunk, Haze, and Northern Lights. Yes, Jack Herer also came from these strains, as did many others. As far as I can tell, the only difference between Jack Herer and Super Silver Haze is that NL5 is the male in the original Super Silver Haze cross, while Haze is the male in Jack's original cross. Jack has a tendency to show a bit of favoritism toward its tall, lanky Haze father. SSH leans more toward the indica side of the spectrum, due to its NL5 father. Quite simply, this is the Dom Perignon of cannabis. Unfortunately, these buds didn't burn properly, as with most Amsterdam herb. A joint wouldn't stay lit, and a bowl ended up as a black chunky carbon-looking thing, not very enjoyable to smoke. Had this strain been grown with love, organically and preferably outdoors, it would have been unbeatable.

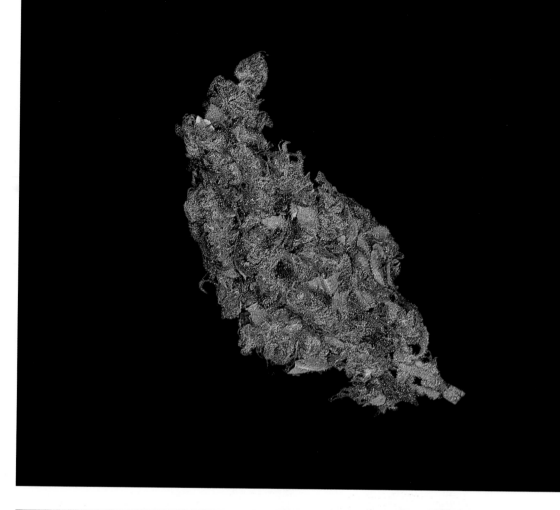

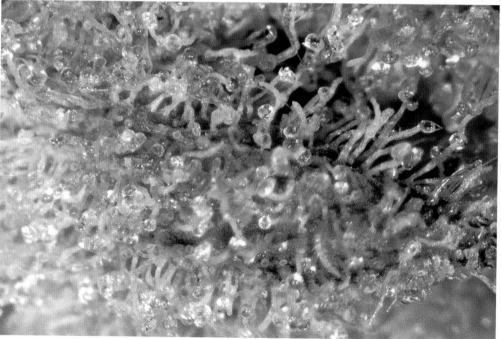

GATE 28

KLM

FLIGHT 602

TO AMSTERDAM

DEPARTS 4:20 PM

The Amsterdam Experience

As anyone who's been there knows, every marijuana enthusiast owes it to him or herself to make at least one pilgrimage to the so-called stoner mecca, Amsterdam. The enticing smell of cannabis drifts through the streets of this fine city, where small amounts of pot and hash can be purchased over the counter at any of the over 1,500 "coffee shops" that grace the city. Officially, these herbs are illegal, but they are tolerated to the point that if you're not being a complete jerk, you will not be hassled. Because of the loose attitude toward cannabis, there is a proliferation of strains available, and one can easily assemble an outrageous collection of nugs and hash in an afternoon by visiting a few good coffee shops. Amsterdam parties like no other city. Nowhere else have I experienced such a variety of entertainment at any given moment. Whether it's live jazz or a pounding rave scene you're looking for, it's always happening in the 'Dam. Summer visits are preferable, as winters are pretty cold. (I don't care how high you are, when you hit that 30-degree bone-chilling air, you are instantly sober. Talk about a buzz-kill!) The feeling of not having to hide your ganja smoking is profoundly liberating and proves how absurd and unnecessary our drug laws are. (Holland has lower teen drug-use statistics than America.) Kudos to the Dutch for having a sane and logical attitude toward their drug laws!

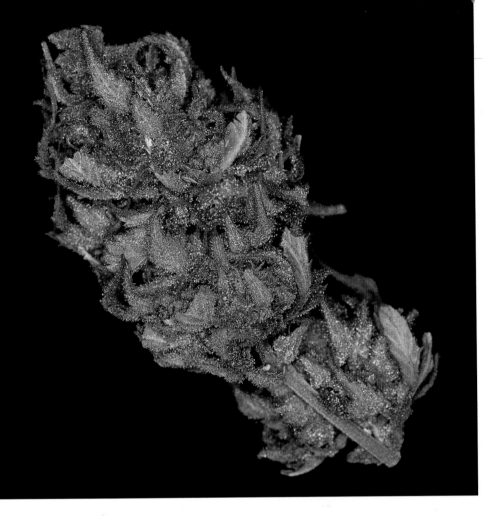

172

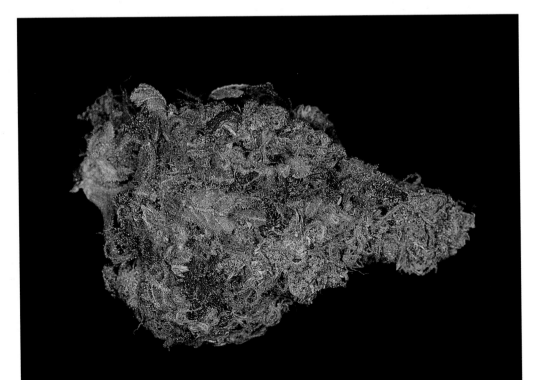

SUPER SKUNK

This mega-hybrid was developed over a period of fifteen years by taking a particularly strong Skunk No. 1 plant and recrossing it with its Afghani ancestors. Almost every coffee shop in Amsterdam has this variety, as it is easy to grow and produces very weighty buds. This plant is extremely sweet tasting, contrary to its name. (The Skunk used to make it must have been the typical Amsterdam sweet variety.) Its potency is above average, yet generic and unfocused. For some unknown reason, I rarely see buds like these in America. I can't complain, as this is not one of my favorite strains. Also pictured is the same (Sensi Seeds) strain grown outdoors organically on Maui (opposite page, upper left). Unlike the Amsterdam-grown buds, the Maui version was tastier and burned properly.

TAHOE OUTDOOR

This magnificent specimen (right) exhibits almost every color in the rainbow, and luckily it tastes as good as it looks. Grown outdoors at over 9,000 feet near Lake Tahoe in California, this bud made my mouth water before I even tried it. There is something very special about high-elevation marijuana. It's not just that it's stronger; it's the character of the high. Clean, clear, and very mind-expanding, this bud brought my brain to places rarely experienced. It is virtually psychedelic. Highly recommended for skiing and other mountain sports.

THAIDAL WAVE

Here is an interesting Thai/Skunk hybrid that is quite delicious. The flavor of the Thai really came through here, a sweet anise sensation. This nearly pure sativa has a trippy, clear high that is very analytical in nature. This plant was grown in a greenhouse in Holland.

THAITANIC

This Flying Dutchmen strain (below) is another fine example of an F1 Thai hybrid that combines two distinctly different gene pools. Hybrid vigor has been achieved here, and the best of both worlds is clearly expressed. Mostly sativa in appearance and high with the quicker indica flowering times, this mostly sativa bud will finish before being frozen. The Thai flavor is extremely sweet and enjoyable, and the clear, up high is wonderful (and was greatly appreciated after a day of indica-inspired fuzziness).

TOP 44

This Dutch-bred mostly indica strain gets its name and reputation for its incredibly fast flowering time. In only forty-four days, she's totally mature. Unfortunately, that's all she's noteworthy for. I found this herb to be extremely generic and quite boring. If you are growing it, please stop. Thank you.

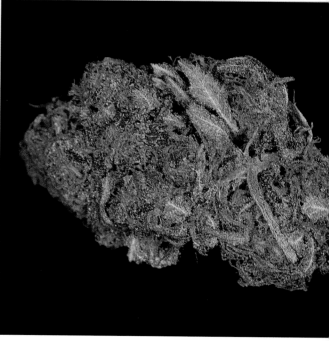

TRINITY

These are easily some of the most pungent nuggets I have ever come across. The overwhelming Skunk odor is so strong that even a sealed jar won't contain it. If you get pulled over with this stuff in your car, you might as well just hand it over to the cop, because there will be no denying what's in the car! ("No, honestly, officer, I just accidentally ran over five hundred skunks at once!") This herb was scored in Eugene, Oregon, where it commanded a higher price than just about any other herb around. If that weren't enough, this particularly greedy grower sells it soaking wet! The desperate connoisseurs still buy it all up, sending a message to the grower that it is okay to sell this herb wet and overpriced. I do not support these actions. Shame on him! As far as genetics go, I have been informed that the Trinity is a three-way cross of select West Coast genetics. This bud produces a knockout buzz and leaves a skunky taste on the palate for hours.

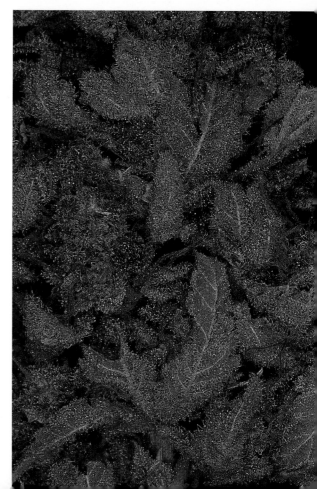

WARLOCK

This strain, scored at the Blue Bird coffee shop in Amsterdam, has received a lot of attention recently. After winning a Cannabis Cup, the connoisseur circle of smokers is becoming more familiar with the name Warlock. She's a Skunk variety, with a full-bodied flavor hinting of flowers and sap. Deep below is a scrumptious sandalwood flavor. The high is very strong, able to bump you up a notch higher than the average bud will take you. This sample was grown indoors in Amsterdam, using the bio method.

WHITE AFGHANI

This hybrid is a cross of White Widow and Afghani #1. My sample veered toward the White side. Overall, I found it to be boring and generic. But then, I never was a huge fan of the White line.

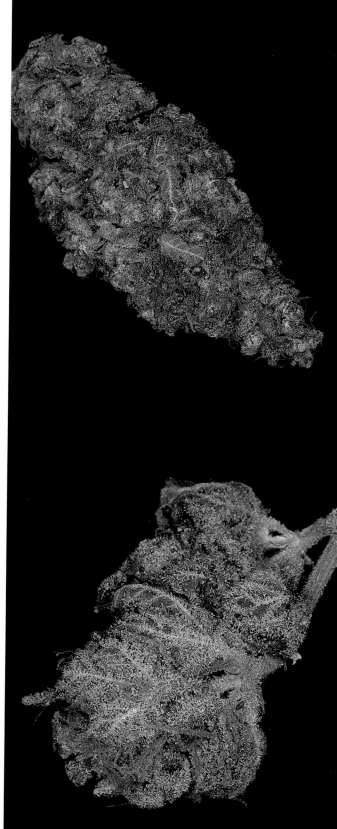

WHITE CHOCOLATE (ALBINO HP13)

This freakish strain was created by crossing HP13 (see page 75) and Purple Northern Lights. The interesting thing about this strain is the albino hairs that will never turn red—this bud is completely mature! The HP13's intense skunky flavor is there, albeit not as strong as a pure HP13. I found the high to be intense, if not nervous and frantic, probably due to the crazy vibration associated with its being grown in New York City.

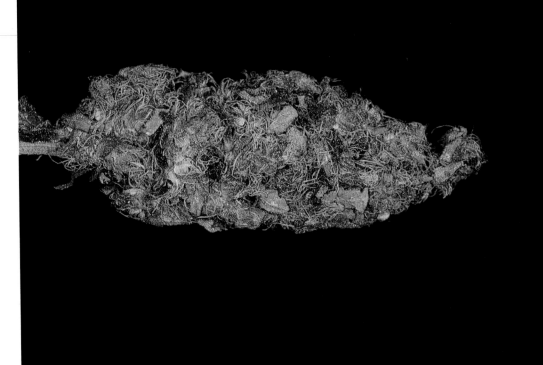

WHITE LADY

White Widow, when crossed with a nice fat Master Kush, produced this lady. Lots of small to medium resin glands team up to produce a deep, heavy stone. The flavor is typical of that from the White line, with an added fruity tang. This batch was biologically grown. (In Amsterdam, this means soil grown—not necessarily organic.)

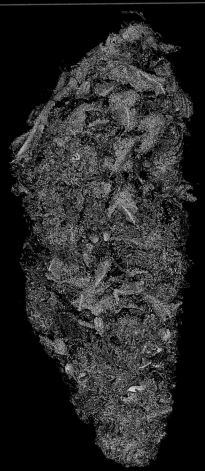

WHITE K.C.

This chunky crustacean of a nugget is a member of the K.C. Brains Holland seed company. The ancestors are a male K.C. 606 and a real White Lady, whatever that means. I found the flavor to be quite nice, halfway resembling sandalwood, although it could have been stronger. The high is warm and fuzzy.

WHITE RHINO

White Rhino is a 60 percent indica/40 percent sativa hybrid offered by the Greenhouse Seed Company. The lineage is something like this: Afghani x Brazilian/South Indian. There are deep and subtle familiar old flavors in there, provided the bud is grown organically so you can distinguish them. Beautiful Alpine-flower fragrances, with subtle sweet and sour aftertones delight the palate. Of the many White family hybrids, this is one of the better ones.

WHITE RUSSIAN

White Russian is a hybrid cross of two of the more famous strains in Amsterdam, AK-47 (see page 28) and White Widow (see page 184). The buds are plump and sweet, with a fruity and somewhat, for lack of a better word, cheesy aroma. Shown is an Amsterdam indoor bio. The batch was pretty good, but I'll take outdoor any day.

WHITE WIDOW

After having won a Cannabis Cup in Amsterdam, this Greenhouse Seed Company–strain has received a lot of attention in the last few years. Most of the coffee shops in Amsterdam now sell a White Widow variety, although a lot of them are questionable. It is rumored that a seed company in competition with the breeders of this strain stole a vegetative cutting at an exhibition and produced seeds with it. This could explain the many other companies selling Widow in a slightly altered form (with something other than Widow as the male). Known for its instability, White Widow is reportedly an Indian x Brazilian, expressed as 60 percent sativa, 40 percent indica. This plant has a soft herbal bouquet, with a light, but in my opinion, boring, flavor. The high is sedative and cloudy. Some commercial Dutch growers are rumored to stress these plants (by running ice water through the hydroponic system, for example) to give them an extra-white appearance. Scary.

WILLIAMS WONDER

I have heard many conflicting stories about Williams Wonder. One expert claimed that it was bred in the United States, while another says that it's an original Dutch variety with little if any U.S. influence. I can't say for sure either way. What I do know is that this short and squat strain packs a pronounced euphoric buzz that I felt mostly in my head. The 1987–1988 Super Sativa Seed Club catalog states that it cannot be flowered outdoors unless flowering is induced inside first, so it is probable that this indica hybrid was selected solely for indoor growing.

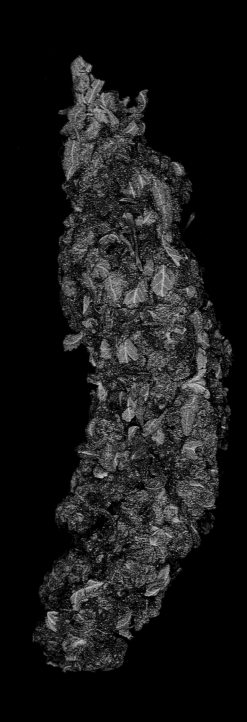

Index

Afterword

As I sit here, just days before *The Cannabible* goes to print, I still have a list of almost 300 strains that are not included in the book. Did I do an inadequate job? Not even close. The more strains I photograph, the more strains I hear about. It seems every person I mention *The Cannabible* to quickly rattles off a list of twenty-five strains that *The Cannabible* would absolutely be incomplete without. More often than not, very few, if any, are included in the book! This is simply a testament to just how many *Cannabis* strains are in existence. With your continued support, I vow to keep on documenting strains (and sampling them!) until *The Cannabible,* Volume 420 comes out over a foot thick! Namaste!